COVID, Cancer, and Christ

COVID, Cancer, and Christ

MATTHEW JOHNSON

RESOURCE *Publications* · Eugene, Oregon

COVID, CANCER, AND CHRIST

Resource Publications
An Imprint of Wipf and Stock Publishers
199 W. 8th Ave., Suite 3
Eugene, OR 97401

www.wipfandstock.com

PAPERBACK ISBN: 978-1-6667-0820-2
HARDCOVER ISBN: 978-1-6667-0821-9
EBOOK ISBN: 978-1-6667-0822-6

11/15/21

Scripture quotations are taken from the BIBLE VERSION PERMISSION.

To my father, Ryan, to my mother, Jennifer, to my brothers, Andrew Jacob and Luke, and to my sister, Emma—

Thank you all for putting up with years of me singing show tunes at unholy hours of the morning, for loving me despite my many shortcomings, and for staying by my side through the best and worst of times. I love you all.

Even though I walk through the valley of the shadow of death,

I fear no evil, for You are with me;

Your rod and Your staff, they comfort me.

—PSALM 23:4 NASB

Contents

Preface

Hello, dear and esteemed reader. I am happy you are reading this; otherwise, there would have been no point in me writing this. So thank you for ensuring that my writing did not go in vain. If you don't know who I am before reading this, you will get to know me through this. My name is Matthew Johnson, and I am a human. I am a man, nineteen years of age at the time I am starting this, an ex-football player, a radio play-by-play announcer, podcaster, food consumption advocate, newspaper writer, winner of a school pageant, theater actor, class of 2020 graduate, cancer survivor, child of a divorced home, American, and much more. Ultimately, I am a Christian, which makes everything else about me pale in comparison. I won the award for doing the most thinking in fifth grade, so you know I am legitimate, and when you sprinkle my life experience in there, I hope that it lends me enough credibility that you will listen to my story—one human to another.

Throughout my walk in life it has been the wisdom of others, be it those with doctorates or those who never graduated high school, that has helped me through some of my most trying times. So that is what I will be attempting to do myself. I am here to share my ever-growing story with you and take you on the journey that I have been on in the past year of my life. I have wrestled a lot, but I hope that through my wrestling and struggles others may be helped. When I first began writing this project, it had been just over a year since COVID-19 began to wreak havoc on the globe. You will see that, like for many in the world, it has been a crazy year for me. Oftentimes we find ourselves in hard situations and it always seems that when it rains it pours, and 2020–2021 was no exception. However, even in the darkest of storms sunlight is on the other side. Even when we cannot see it. Without further ado, I hope you enjoy reading through my story of COVID, cancer, and Christ.

Acknowledgments

This book is the product of many conversations that I had during and after my cancer treatments. Without these conversations and the encouragement to put pen to paper, this book would not exist.

To my mom, Jennifer, and my dad, Ryan,

I thank you both for loving me so well not only this year but throughout my life. You have encouraged me in my pursuits, corrected me when I needed it, and raised me in the way I ought to go. You both have always selflessly served me and cared for me more than yourselves. Thank you for all of the laughter, compassion, encouragement, and love that each of you has shown to me throughout the years. Not only were you there for me in the darkest of times, but you were there to make the memories I consider to be the best of times. You have been patient with me, showing kindness throughout my life. You have never envied anything from me nor boasted of yourselves, but have always honored me as higher than yourselves. You have not been easily angered and do not keep record of my wrongs. You have loved me. And love never fails.

To my sister, Emma,

Thank you for always being a terrific sister to me. You are very loved and cherished by me. If you ever need a reminder, call me and we can discuss it over some doughnuts. If someone were to replace you with a fake sister, I would reject that fake sister and find you, my real sister.

To my brother, Luke,

Thank you for always loving and caring for me. I enjoy each and every time I get to see you and it has been an honor watching you go from a small baby just a few days old to where you are now. I am excited to see who you grow up to become. While we spend a great deal of time apart, know that you always have a place close to my heart.

To my brother, Andrew Jacob,

Thank you for being my brother. You have always humbled me with how big your heart for others is and I strive to love as you love. From the time you were a monkey swinging on the plants in our house to now, you have always been there with me through thick and thin. From every backyard action movie shoot that I dragged you along for, to when I told you to fall without bracing the landing, you have always been by my side. You have been my constant in life and you have always defended me when you thought I was in danger. Even if you did try to defend me as a tiger. I will always be able to tell when someone knew us by what they call you. To those in Kentucky and before, you are Jacob. After we moved back to Alabama, AJ. But no matter what combination of Andrew Jacob you call yourself in the future, I will always know you as my brother whom I cherish. I love you very much.

To my grandfather, Gary "Peepaw" Johnson,

I could not have asked for a better grandfather. You have always been the picture of a godly man to me and I know that the process of becoming one has been a lifelong journey for you. I remember riding around on your knee as we rode through your yard on the lawn mower or the tractor. I remember going fishing and throwing the football. I remember our long deep discussions when we got to see you and Meemaw. I remember the hard work ethic you helped instill in both Andrew Jacob and me. I do not think I will ever forget listening to your old stories of the farm and your time in the navy. I love you, Peepaw. I know your father all those years ago may have told you that you would not amount to anything, but hear it louder from your grandson that you have. And not only have you amounted to something, but you have amounted to many great things, only one of which is being a terrific grandfather to me.

To my grandmother, Candy "Meemaw" Johnson,

Thank you for being a wonderful grandmother to me. You have always made sure that all of your grandkids know they are loved and that they never leave your house wanting. Whether it be the best milkshakes from the old antique milkshake machine, or the massive dinners and delicious desserts, you have always served us even when it wasn't your favorite thing to do. I am pretty sure that the only reason I love Fruit Loops is because I could always look forward to them at your house. Thank you for always loving me. I will always love you.

To my grandmother, Kathy "Meega" Harmon,

You may not be one for sentimental words, but that is okay because actions speak louder than words and you are a woman of action. When things break, you are there to fix them. When someone is in need, you do not just talk about helping them—you do it. You instilled a hard work ethic in your grandchildren and you always backed up that hard work with fun play. I always know that if I need you, you will be there about thirty minutes early. You are deeply loved by me and I thank you for being my grandmother.

To my uncles, Josh and Eric, my aunts, Amber and Jenny, and my cousins, August, Elie, Myers, and Amelia,

Thank you all for the support you have given me throughout this year, but more so thank you for all of the great memories I have gotten to make with all of you. You are all dearly missed whether you are in the same state, a mile high in Denver, or an ocean away. I look forward to the time I get to be with you all again.

To my friend and brother in Christ, Denson Gould,

Words cannot express how thankful I am for you. You were the first person to mention that I should make a book, and while you may not have had a hand in crafting it, you are just as much responsible for it as anyone else. While much of the eyeballs have been on me, you have been diligently going through trials of your own as you have had to deal with your roommate suddenly leaving for a month, and then staying by my side throughout the long months of chemotherapy, caring for me as a true brother would. I cannot express how grateful I am to have been sharpened by your wisdom and spurred on by your zeal to know God above all else. I am honored to call you my friend.

To all the doctors, nurses, and healthcare professionals at Auburn Pediatric and Adult Medicine and the University of Alabama in Birmingham Hospital,

I cannot thank you all enough. I have no doubt that without the swift action taken to get me admitted, the professionalism and brilliance that I was shown throughout my treatment, and the kindness along with compassion that I was shown from my doctors down to the nurses, I would not be here today. I owe my life to you all and I thank you very much.

To my missional community from 2020–2021,

Thank you all for walking alongside me through what was easily one of the hardest times in my life. The first semester we grew close so that when the second semester rolled around I knew I could lean on each of you when I needed it. So thank you Jimbo and Kat Alldredge, Abby Thomas, Caleb McLeod, Claire Sission, David Kuykendall, Denson Gould, Jack Singley, Jacob and Sarah Istre, Jake Farris, Luke Barker, Olivia Schaffner, Reed Henderson, Sally Kicklighter, Sarah Grace Sapp, and Tyler Bottomlee.

To my pastor, Will Spivey,

You were one of the first calls I received when I was diagnosed even though you did not know me well at the time. I remember that you were the first person to publicly announce my diagnosis when you told the college ministry on the day I began chemotherapy. You were the one to baptize me a few months later once I was able to leave the hospital. From that time on you have always been diligent in speaking with me and making me feel known and cared for while still running one of, if not the, largest student ministries in our area. I thank you for loving, advising, and serving as a follower of Christ.

To Jimbo and Kat Alldredge, Earvin Comer, Dean Jones, and Owen Meadows,

Thank you for being the first ones to take a look at what would later become this book. Your feedback and encouragement are what inspired me to take this book farther than a mere document of my thoughts sitting on my computer.

To Hannah Holliday,

Thank you for your invaluable feedback, which helped shape this book from rough draft into a cohesive document that will hopefully help many. Your encouragement means the world to me.

To those who prayed for and donated to my family and me,

I tried to go back and create an all-inclusive list encompassing every name that prayed and gave, but I simply could not. The amount of prayer I received was overwhelming and I am humbled and beyond thankful for each and every one of you who took the time to advocate for my family and me through prayer or through generous giving.

To Owen Meadows, Jack Smith and Jeromy Swann,

Thank you three for being alongside me throughout this year as you all have poured into me spiritually and intellectually. Thank you all for the wisdom that was passed from you to me that has permeated the page. While none of you may be directly quoted, your thoughts have certainly helped better this book.

To all of my friends,

As you will read in this book, I value few things more than relationships. To all of my close friends now and throughout the years, thank you. You have brought me some of the best memories and laughs. You came and visited me while I was in the hospital, even if it was from eight stories down through a glass window. I cannot begin to tell you how much little gestures like that mean to me. Thank you all.

To the publishing team,

Thank you for believing in this book and putting in all the hard work of turning this project into a creation I get to hold with my hands. It would not have been possible without all of you fine folks at Wipf and Stock.

BOOK ONE

COVID

"Normal" Life

In February of 2020, I had just returned from a theater trip in Nashville, Tennessee. I was taking the trip with my girlfriend at the time, my future roommate, and one of our very good friends, with my dear mother as the chaperone. It was my third such trip and it would be my last. Graduation was just a few months away, so I knew I had to savor the experience. Life would be different soon as high school was dwindling to a close and shortly after I would be moving off to college, but I was excited. I had a good set of friends around me, I was taking fun trips away from school to do what I loved to do, and I was getting ready to audition and perform in my final show as a theater actor. I had done theater all four years of my high school career, so it was especially important for me to prepare to make sure this one last show would have meaning and be my best one yet. As I reminisced about past years, I couldn't help but mourn the fond memories and the people I had grown to know, knowing they would not be with me forever. However, I was filled with excitement. I had planned the speeches I meant to make in our final cast circle and prepared harder for the audition than ever before, and I was confident in my plans to go out with a bang, get my high school diploma, and begin college in just a few short months. The closing months of a high schooler's career are some of the busiest, with award celebrations and senior events galore. This was a time with so many new things on the horizon that I could not help but be a little excited as visions of college life and independence flashed across my mind. Little did I—or anyone, for that matter—realize how different life would be in just a year.

It is easy to look back and think of that pre-COVID era as a time of bliss, but let me tell you a little secret: it was not. In preparation for these writings, I came across a note that I had journaled to myself following the auditions for *Little Shop of Horrors*, my last theater show. I had high expectations for myself but I had failed to get the lead role. Looking back, it was the right casting decision, but allow me to let you in on my thoughts at the time-

I have tried and tried to find the best thoughts to focus on but it is hard. I am a dad/dad role for the seventh or eighth show in the past four years. I lost the lead role, and had to tell everyone who was excited for me, everyone telling me I'd make a great plant, that I didn't get the part. That's friends, family, even coworkers. It's the icing on the cake of what has been a hard year for my esteem.

It's hard to know that I have seen no reward or benefit for all my time in the last four years. By the time I am done, I will have been in thirteen shows and have only played the lead male in one of them. I am the only one left from my freshman class. They've all left. So I do feel lonely too because of that. I have memories no one else cares about.

Little Shop is yet another show. There's no room to improve anymore. No next show to audition for. This was it. And I have failed. Again. I seem to be very good over the course of my life at two things: one of them is getting close to people just to lose them, and two is disappointing people. I miss the friendships of theater. I love the people. I have so many great memories. But when it comes to my own personal development, I have been a flop.

I only hope that my career will be different. To make lasting relationships. To matter.

There is so much I could comment about that writing from a year ago that I could probably write an entirely separate book in response, but for the purpose of this chapter I want to focus on the broad picture. Oftentimes I, in this post-pandemic world, look back on "normal" life and see it as a time of bliss, where my troubles were few and far between. But that is just a lie. I had issues of self-esteem, doubt, feeling like a failure—all of this over a theater career. A high school theater career at that.

What I find most interesting looking back on what I wrote, although it was from a vulnerable state of distress, are the things that I was focused on to give myself meaning. I think it has been one of the places where I have been severely flawed. I need to remember that even when life felt normal and under control, I still had deeply rooted issues and flaws. Perhaps the pandemic did not create in me the issues I have struggled with over this past year, but rather it may very well be possible that it adjusted the lens for me to see the already-existing flaws in my way of life. Still, it is hard to look back and remember what it felt like to have all of the comforts of that "normal" life—to be preparing for graduation and college, to be hanging out with friends without talk of masks or vaccinations—and not miss that time just a little.

What was "normal" life for me? Well, it was the daily grind of ensuring that I woke up in the morning, antagonized my siblings, got to school on time enough to talk to my girlfriend before class started, walked her in, performed the morning announcements, completed my classes, helped out with the kids at an extended-day program, returned to school for theater, and got home by ten to do homework. And then do it all over again the next day. Fourteen hours away from home was no stranger to me, but, while it was tiring, I was doing things that I loved so I did not care. I enjoyed being busy and I felt like many of the things I was doing had significance. On the weekends I would hang out with my group of friends and many nights we would have a fun game or movie night, and those I miss very much.

I love plans and being in a rhythmic pattern of life and I made plans quite often. In fact, I even have a plan for how to eat Oreos (always in pairs, one to eat regularly and the other to break open and eat the cream first and then the cookies). Even when I had free time, I made sure to schedule in exactly when in my day that free time would be. I can so easily tell you the pattern of my days because that is exactly what it was for months and months and I was quite comfortable with it being that way. That rhythm is quite simply what normal life was for me. So, aside from the occasional trip or vacation that interrupted my usual flow of life, you now have a clear picture of what my life looked like heading into March of 2020. However, you can already see how all of the plans that I held near and placed my hope in failed me. I was devastated when my plan to succeed in theater failed to come to fruition, but little did I realize just how much my vision for the future was about to undergo a catastrophic transformation.

The Missing Chapter

In March of 2020, America was stunned as life was seemingly brought to a halt. I remember where I was when it was announced that COVID-19 had become a pandemic, but up to that time not much had changed in my life. I remember thinking to myself that this was probably just another scare. I was in seventh grade around the time the Ebola outbreak happened, and while we heard a lot about it in the news, it never actually affected our daily lives, so I figured COVID would probably end up being the same thing. I understood how COVID could infect a crowded country like China, or an underdeveloped country with little resources, but the United States had always felt largely invincible from these widespread scares.

When we were let out for spring break, I remember that there was talk of potentially postponing school by a week or so, but that at the time was seen as improbable because of the audacity and rarity of such a notion. No teacher at that time had ever experienced such a long shutdown. What the teachers had experienced, though, was an event in American history known as 9/11, and in many circles that is what the fear of the oncoming COVID pandemic was being compared to. The only issue was that 9/11 happened in a day and though the effects have permeated life to this day, especially in the airline industry, the gravity of the event has, rather sadly, steadily been lost. That is to say that the fear of being attacked by terrorists on American soil has not been on the everyday mind of the average American. But COVID was not something that would happen in a day. Please do not think that I am undermining the weight of 9/11, but rather realize that I am emphasizing how much weight that event had on America. We were all realizing that what we were about to face was no small event. The looming situation was so big, in fact, that what many considered to be the most traumatic event in the average American adult memory at the time was the only thing people had to compare it to. Even 9/11 did not shut Alabama schools down for a week, but that was what was being considered.

As we drove away from the school on what was—although unknown to us—our last day ever of high school, we did not take the threat of a school shutdown seriously. As one administrator pointed out prior to us leaving, there was more at stake than just educational functions. Our school is a low-income public school, meaning that a certain number of residents in the city qualified for food assistance due to their income level. This means the school system provides meals to those students free of charge. For those with solid incomes, food is no problem. But there are many children whose only pathway to consistent food is through the school system, and if the school system shuts down they will be at an even greater risk of food insecurity. This reality was just one of the many things on the minds of the school officials as shutdowns were being considered.

I went on my way to Disney World as a part of my spring break trip. I was excited because it was going to be my third time going and I hadn't been there in nearly a decade. I realized how rare even that was for many families, so I was extremely appreciative of the chance to go. It had been announced that Disney World would be closing due to the pandemic, which was a huge deal seeing as how it would become the longest shutdown in Disney World history, but I was going right until the day it closed. I had a blast on the trip, determined to enjoy the rare opportunity to the best of my abilities. However, it was becoming more and more apparent that my normal way of life was in jeopardy. It didn't take long after my return for the official announcement to be made that our school would not be returning for at least a week or two. That at the time was mind-boggling to us, and we joked that our senior class had outdone ourselves on senior skip day.

As the weeks dragged on and quarantine began, it was clear that the pandemic was not going to resolve in a week or two. I remember where I was standing when the announcement was made by Alabama Governor Kay Ivey that schools would be going virtual for the remainder of the school year. Different events such as senior prom, picnic, award ceremonies, our last theater show, and even graduation were pushed back, redesigned, and ultimately (minus graduation) canceled. Our graduation, an event that every child looks forward to, had a guest list limited to just eight family members per student and was over in thirty seconds. Now, I am not angry at the decisions made over our graduation ceremony. In fact, I think the administrators did a wonderful job and gave us some semblance of a graduation when many schools didn't even do that. However, anyone from the class of 2020 will tell you that it was hard to not have a regular end to our time in school. It was not just graduation, though; it was a whole host of events. It was as if an author had been writing a book for twelve years only to quit at the last chapter. Suddenly all of the things I had been looking forward to and planning on were gone and I was helpless to do anything about it. There was nothing I could do but sit and watch as one thing after another fell.

The situation was quite devastating for me. For the first time, many students began to miss being in school. The big takeaway that I heard many people talking about as the spring and summer months of quarantine stretched on was appreciation. I, and many alongside me, were learning for the first time just how unstable our lives were. My coveted daily routine had vanished and while I tried to fill that time doing other things, none of them compared to what I had hoped to be doing. Very quickly all of my gripes about not getting the specific role in my final show went away as I wished that I had a show to begin with. My frustrations with my schoolwork were overshadowed by my longing to see my friends again before we all moved off to college. I learned very quickly and in a very distressing way that I took a massive amount of comforts in my life for granted. I felt like I had lost everything. All of the things I had been involved in that had been giving me purpose had suddenly gone away and that was a very difficult thing to wrestle with. I felt as though I was wasting my days and that they were purposeless.

As the pandemic swept the nation, I could not help but realize just how much I had been ungrateful for. It is easy to nitpick the little things when you sit at a certain level of comfort, but I hope I never forget that I need to look at the bigger picture. As with my theater disappointment, rather than putting my focus on complaints with the role, I need to focus on gratitude for the show itself.

Nothing to Do

As soon as I heard the news that school was canceled for the rest of the year, I began searching for job openings. I was a busy person and I figured getting a job and saving up money before I became a broke college student would serve me well. My regular job with the extended day program would not be an option, so I cast my net out, looking to find a suitable spring and summer profession. I eventually landed on delivery driving for a pizza restaurant, as well as writing for a local newspaper. Planning to go into college for broadcast journalism, I figured writing for a newspaper would be both a good way to both sharpen my skills as a writer and good experience to list on future resumes.

As I began these two jobs, for the first time in my life I truly experienced what a full-time, no-school work week could be like. Now granted, during the school year I spent more hours away from home, but spending time in school and spending time at work are two very different things. Over the next few months, I quickly became emotionally exhausted. The delivery job gave me as close to forty hours a week as they could and they often scheduled me for shifts that I had specifically requested to be off. When you throw the newspaper job on top of that and the fact that I was trying to maintain good relationships with my girlfriend and family, both of whom were completely free all day, you can imagine how the stress began to mount.

For a time I was determined to buckle down and work both jobs, but the pizza delivery job was not cutting down my hours. They were too short-staffed to afford to. My week consisted of working eight-to-ten-hour shifts all but two days of the week, and when I got off I would try to go over to my girlfriend's house. Early on in quarantine, her family did movie marathons that started when I got there and when the movie was over I left. I say that to note that although I was spending time with her, we were not talking or getting quality time. Then on my two days off I would try to spend quality time with her, but with most places being shut down, it meant we were resigned to mostly indoor activities or going for walks. Those were nice at first but after months on end they became repetitive. The situation was also taking a toll on my relationship with my family as I was often never home. We could not have our usual game and movie nights with friends either, as quarantine orders prevented us from seeing groups of people.

I had made myself busy again, but I had both sides of the people I cared about, my girlfriend and my family, consistently saying they did not feel like they were having enough of my time. It is a good problem to have, to be wanted, but eventually it causes a strain and something has to give. I eventually crunched the numbers and figured that I could make ends meet through my newspaper job, which only required about ten to twenty hours a week. I could also do that work from home. So I left my delivery job once they started hiring more drivers and then I had much more time on my hands.

That was the first time in my life that I ever experienced what it was like to have free time, except for maybe when I was a kid. You might think of summer as a time of freedom for a kid, but even then I was always staying busy by either spending most of my time with my dad or taking trips and doing activities with my family. I had never had nothing to do before. For years I had always been enveloped with so many activities and now there was nothing, besides calling people for interviews and writing news articles—that I could do. One would think that with this newfound time the issue of juggling my time between my family and my significant other would have subsided, but instead it changed into a new issue: too much free time.

I enjoy a busy life, and I did not realize how much I did until I no longer had anything to do. Some of my friends still to this day consider those quarantine months to be the best time in their lives, but I do not. Instead, I did not have a routine, and I went from the extreme of having almost no time with my girlfriend to the extreme of too much time. It is always interesting to me how often and in how many different areas of our lives we tend to correct one extreme by swinging the pendulum over to the other extreme. Now my predicament became spending days with my girlfriend, which put a strain on my relationship with my family, and then on the days where I spent time at home with my family, nobody did anything much. I began to experience how awful I was at having free time.

Now, outside circumstances certainly factored into my issues. If there had been different activities to do around the area—a pool to go swim in, perhaps, or even a restaurant to dine in—just to break up the monotony of life, I believe that would have helped. Instead, what we experienced was repetitive boredom and the same scenery again and again. I remember having told myself throughout the years I was busy, "If only I had more free time, then I could get so much more accomplished." Perhaps there are some out there who truly lived that out, but for me that could not have been farther from the truth. I became, quite honestly, very lazy. It was difficult to get motivated to do anything when you were stuck at home for months on end. I had always operated in life looking forward to something. For example, I might say, "I just have to make it two more weeks before we open the show; I can make it through this math class until then." I now see how flawed I was in this way of thinking. I wasted a lot of meaningful time by wishing it away until the next event I was excited for, instead of making the most of all the time I was given.

My affection for looking to future events was not getting me through quarantine as I was used to. The very next thing I had to look forward to was moving out and that wasn't going to happen for months. Even then it was a question whether the realty company would be ready for us to move in on time. I spent months not having much to do and I wrestled heavily with that. I could be lazy and relax for maybe a day or two, but for weeks and months I could not. It drove me crazy. Eventually, at the beginning of July, my girlfriend and I broke up, which was devastating to me emotionally and gave me even more free time on my hands. My family was able to take a short trip out to Colorado to see my uncle and his family, which I greatly enjoyed, but there were still weeks left before I moved out to college and now there would be no issue with being at home with my family because that is all I could do.

By July, my friends and I were finally able to hang out once again, so I saw them occasionally, but the majority of my days were spent alone and with massive amounts of free time and I did not know what to do. I would like to say that after those months I eventually came to a grand solution and was no longer bothered by free time, but that is just not the case. I only stopped struggling with free time once college began and my busy life once again resumed. But I was able to see now, for the first time in my life, just how much I relied on my busy schedule and how much comfort I found in it. And even though while I was busy I craved free time, I now knew just how much harder free time can end up being for me. My battle with free time would rear its head again in the near future, but we will get to that later.

A Softened Heart

To rewind a few years, I got my first girlfriend when I was a freshman in high school, my second the year after, and my third through my junior and senior years. All three of them taught me very valuable lessons both about myself and about the world at large. The first taught me that dating someone just because they claim to like you may not be the best idea. The second raised a mirror in my face about many of my own faults. Looking back, I realize how much I was willing to sacrifice in the name of making another happy. I also am saddened by my own actions and how I treated her. I dated her through my father's second divorce, which caused me to be very worn out. Unfortunately, I took that out on her and I regret that very much. But the third taught me more than perhaps anyone else.

It is important to note that I hold the relationship between myself and my significant other very highly. As I will discuss, at times I think I have held the relationship too highly, but I can never be accused of not caring for and investing in my significant other. As a child, my parents divorced at a young age and my father's second divorce was between my freshman and sophomore year of high school. Because of those divorces, I often swore to myself that I would make the relationships I am a part of work. I say this so you will realize that when I entered a relationship I did so headlong, taking the whole thing much more seriously than I think many high schoolers do. It is also important to bear in mind that I have felt very lonely for most of my life, something I will address more later on, but keep that in mind. It wasn't until about my junior year of high school that I had a consistent group of friends that I hung out with regularly. So, prior to my junior year of high school, whoever I was dating was often the only friend I had at the time, the only one I talked to, and the only one outside of my family that I spent time with. That much meaning in one person could cause several issues, as I am sure you can foresee.

When I entered my relationship with my most recent girlfriend, we spent a lot of time together. This was the first girlfriend that I could spend time with. The first I only dated for two months and rarely saw her, and the second lived an hour away. So this time I was learning how to handle a relationship where I was in person more than over text. It is hard to encompass all of our year-and-a-half relationship into concise pages, but I will say that for a long time, even as I look back now, I think it was a good relationship. Neither of us were perfect but we both did care for one another.

Unfortunately, many of those good dynamics changed once COVID hit. While I was working, I was gone for quite a bit, causing issues as we hardly spent any time around one another. Then when I left the pizza delivery business, I was there often. However, rather than being able to do things in the presence of one another, there was very little to do but stare at each other's faces. This provided the perfect grounds to, as time went on, address some of those issues we had previously failed to deal with and create some new ones. Eventually, our relationship slowly began to degrade as issues arose, and distance was created.

Our communication also slowly began to break down as both of us began to feel less comfortable being truly open with one another. When you are in a relationship and the ability to talk openly and freely goes away, it is a recipe for disaster. Despite our growing list of issues, I, being the forward-looking person that I am, saw our situation as a rough patch and thought that it could probably improve once quarantine ended and a regular pace of life resumed. Of course that's what I thought. I was comfortable when I had a rhythmic pace of life and I figured our issues would resolve once we could get comfortable again. Except that I was looking forward to *my* definition of comfortable.

When the breakup came, I realized that our friend group, which was the same at the time, would change. So while I was losing my best friend, I also felt I was losing my friend group, and while I have still maintained good relationships with them all, it has never been quite the same. Not because they took sides, but rather because it was always difficult for me to find my new place whenever we did hang out. So in one day I lost my best friend as well as the friend group I had loved. I could describe the pain in hindsight but I think it would be better if I let the words of my past self describe what I was feeling in the moment:

> I am lonely. Within two weeks I have lost my girlfriend, my best friend, and my friend group. And now just two weeks later I'm already tired of being the one to have to reach out to people.

> The person who understands me the most wants no contact from me. No one else tries. If I stopped reaching out to people no one would ever talk to me and I would truly be alone.
>
> I just want to be wanted by someone. I'd love it if it was someone I wanted too. I miss my best friend. I am not missed. That is why I am typing this. Because I have no one else.

I would like to note that I did have a good friend who was by my side throughout the first few days and I am forever thankful for that support; however, nothing he could have done would have been equivalent to the friend I had just lost. Loneliness is, in my opinion, one of the most severe pains one can go through, and that is why I will be writing about it more later.

I still regard significant-other relationships to be some of the most important ones there are. The ability to truly know someone and to selflessly serve them, putting oneself aside for another, is incredible to me. It also gives so many examples of the relationship we are to have with Christ. I do think the church ought to emphasize single lifestyles more than they do and marriage wrongly feels like the main goal in life for many people. Some, like I used to, spend their days with thoughts and prayers begging God for a significant other. But it is not a significant other who solves our innermost issues. Just go ask any married couple. Rather, I truly believe that until single people surrender their purpose from being about finding a partner, and instead focus on serving God, whether they marry or not, they will not be satisfied. I do not say that lightly, but in reality I say that to myself.

The ability to intimately know another person and to truly love and to be loved is a tremendous thing and when done right is quite beautiful. That is also why it is so painful when a romantic relationship fails. With the great possibility of reward comes the possibility of failure, and as beautiful as relationships can be when done right, they can be just as ugly when done wrong. I am certainly not qualified to write a guide on how to make them work, but I am a person who is always learning from the mistakes of myself, my past relationships, and those of my parents. I hope that one day I will have the opportunity to have another relationship and to conduct that relationship in a serving manner. I do think that in the past I have placed my complete purpose, as many do, in that other person. In doing so I have sacrificed relationships with my friends and family that were equally as important to foster and care for. There is a balance and I am still trying to perfect that balance.

Throughout all that happened in those months, I learned a great deal, not just about relationships with significant others, but it drastically changed how I view other people. You see, I used to, rather wrongly, divide the world up into the good people, the so-so people, and the ones who were bad. I would see a person who always tried to do the right thing and adhered to strong morals and never really did much wrong, and I would think that was a good person. I would see people who always tried to do good but perhaps they slipped up and didn't always do the right thing. Then there were the axe murders and child abusers of the world, who were in a bottom league of their own.

I was very convicted of this way of thinking in the months following my breakup. I began to see how wrong these categories are. What I came to learn is that people are not so neatly boxed up, and that it certainly is not the godly way to view people. Everyone, myself included, has too many pitfalls and shortcomings of our own to regard ourselves as better than anyone else, and though we like to view those people who cut us off in traffic as stupid, or we ostracize and degrade in our minds those who annoy or hurt us, that is not how we should view people at all. You see, when you truly are loving someone, you cannot be angry at them in the traditional sense. When there is an unconditional love present, there is room for feeling complex emotions. Anyone with children will understand that it is possible to both unconditionally love your child and be angry with them simultaneously. However, that anger never takes away the value that your child has for you. We are called to love others in the same way. You can pray "God help this person" while thinking this person is a lunatic and secretly hate them in your heart, or you can pray "God help this person" with compassion and pity. The two use the same words but only one is the loving mindset.

Oftentimes we picture pity as someone as being in a higher place looking down on someone, but that is not true pity. True pity comes from compassion, and compassion from love—not that the other person needs to get to my superior place but that I know there exists a better life than the one they are currently living and my soul is saddened that they are not there. For example, a person might look at a criminal and say "I pity you" but in their heart they are degrading that person's value to a place beneath themselves. Contrast that to a parent who has watched their child suffer in some way. A good parent will say "I pity you," but they do not mean that they are in any way superior to their child. Rather, they merely mean they know there is a better state of being for their child that they wish their child were experiencing. I hope I have made the difference between the two clear, because it is a radical difference. It is difficult to describe because of the multiple connotations we give words, but the two mindsets could not be further from one another, and once I began to see *all* people in this new way, my entire view on people changed.

Now some reading this might remark to themselves, "I don't regard people in that way," especially if you consider yourself to be more accepting of a wide variety of moral choices and worldviews. However, I would argue that what I see is that people, regardless of how accepting they claim to be, often sort others, at the very least, between those they like and those they don't like. A person might be rude to you at the store and the reaction of most people is to be rude back, or, if they have some restraint, to bite their tongue and, once they've left, proceed to tell their friends about the rude person in the store. Either way, that rude person will forever be associated with that dark feeling in the heart.

Oftentimes we will take those whom we like and who are close to us and give them grace because we know their background and what makes them tick, and we might even do this to strangers who have not wronged us because we feel no reason to dislike them. However, it is extremely rare to find people who love their enemy. That is because it is completely unnatural. I remember one lady who, when I was working at my pizza delivery job, reported me to the manager because I did not give her enough Parmesan cheese and she became very angry very quickly. To her, anything I did became disrespectful. I bit my tongue and dealt with the situation, and from the surface it appeared as though I handled it respectfully. Some people would have become defensive and snapped back, and I did not do that, so many thought I handled it well. However, for months after the incident I found myself gossiping about it, and if she had walked into the room, I, at least in my heart, would have cast her down and wished that she would go away. There was certainly no love for her in my heart.

Contrast that story to a few weeks ago, when I went into the hospital to get some bloodwork done and I was told by a nurse at the window to sit down. Now, the nurse said this command in such a way that it sounded rude, and it offended quite a few people who came in. They would mutter under their breath their frustration with her and sometimes would audibly huff their way to the seat, only to get back up and go back to the window a minute or two later in frustration. At first, I too was put off by the way she spoke to me, but I decided to bury that frustration and give her the benefit of the doubt. After some time, the nurse called me into the back room, and as she was drawing my blood she proceeded to thank me for simply sitting down. She explained to me her busy day and how things were going wrong at every step and how tired she was in life, and how much my not taking out my frustration on her made her day better. Now, could she have worked on how she spoke? Of course, but it was my loving response to the nurse, as opposed to my unloving response to the pizza customer, that began to make a difference. It is not natural, but it is better.

I was not able to make this change until I watched people whom I love go down pathways that I knew weren't the best for them, and it was then that my eyes were opened as to what it truly means to pity someone but to do so in a loving way. When I started to make this change in how I saw people, it slowly changed my behavior in so many ways. It has snowballed to the point where I cannot even imagine hating someone as I did before. And by "hate" I do not mean it in the usual sense of having dripping, unloving malice towards someone, but I mean simply shunning someone in my heart. We often claim to not hate people, but our hearts tell a different story.

Where I see this scenario play out the most is in the realm of social media. I might see someone, especially if I do not know them, do or say something and automatically go, "That's stupid," and whoever made the comment or did the stupid action in my mind gets their value degraded. This happens all of the time and often subconsciously, but not just on social media. We often do this with people in life. Just think of how many idiots there are in the world from your time driving. And yet, how many times have you made a mistake on the road? I know I have made my fair share. I have probably been labeled an idiot in many people's minds, but I would hope that my value as a person isn't determined by my driving mistakes, so why would I determine others' values in such a way? And yet I do it all the time.

There are also people whose presence would cause me to feel anxiety or anger because of events in the past, but that is not loving my neighbor either. I am called to love all people despite my history with them or whether or not we agree. As I began to see those who hurt me with love and compassion, trying to better understand them as a person and getting to the root of the issue rather than the offense against me, it made all of my friendships deeper and my interactions with people more meaningful. Not to mention that I have become much happier because of it. Now, I do not simply write off all offenses, and people have still hurt me. Loving someone is not always accepting what they do, nor is it always turning a blind eye to offenses, but rather it is caring for them deeply despite what they do. Rather than associating others' value with their treatment of me, I have upheld their value and sorted out their offenses in a loving manner. As a Christian, this is the life I am called to. I don't just tolerate my enemy, but I am called to truly love those who do not show love towards me, even to those who hurt me. That is much harder to do than I think people realize, but it is much more rewarding in the end. The change I am talking about is not a new way of treating people. Most people know how to be kind; they are just selective as to whom they are kind to. The real change I had in my life was in how I saw and valued people. When I have valued and cared for those that have hurt me, it has made a difference in people's lives far beyond what I ever could have imagined. I do not think that many quotes sum it up better than the late doctor, apologist, and cancer-fighter Nabeel Qureshi:

> If you are a follower of Jesus, you should be willing to do what Jesus did. Well, what did Jesus do? He was willing to die for his enemies. The greatest being willing to die the worst death ever devised by humankind. That's what he was willing to do. Do you follow him? Do you love your enemies enough to do that for them? Because that's what it means to follow Christ. If that's how you see the world and that's how you understand people, then you have understood the gospel.[1]

I would also like to take a moment to talk about familial relationships. While I did not have any new ways of seeing them, as I did for people in general, nor did I have any hard lessons with them, as I did when it came to significant others, I think it would be wrong to not mention them briefly, as they are some of my most important relationships. Although my family is broken through a divorce, I would not trade my experiences for a different life. My parents live different lifestyles and run their homes in slightly different ways, but that has allowed me to objectively see the pros and cons of both choices, and I think that has allowed me to live a better life because of it.

Despite my parent's flaws, they have always loved me without fail, and for that I could not think of a luckier person to be than their child. I have never felt unloved or unsupported by either of them. Now, they haven't always thought I was right, but that is a good thing. The most foolish children are the ones whose parents think they can do no wrong. To watch your child go through cancer at nineteen is no small feat, and I am constantly impressed by the skill with which they handle themselves and the love, compassion, selflessness, sacrifice, and support they continue to show me throughout this ordeal. My siblings have grown close to me and I with them, and, despite my not always being the best brother to them, they have always loved me.

In the past, I have not paid attention to my relationship with them as much as I should, but through the best and worst in my life they have always been there for me, and I love them very much and am very thankful for all of them. You can always tell what something is worth to someone by what they are willing to pay for it. I have seen that with my own family and friends, who have paid a tremendous amount for me. I am not merely talking financially, although that is true, but they have also sacrificed time, care, love, and their own well-being for my own. Through the countless nights where family and friends have had to wake up to tend to me, or the month spent in

---

1. Qureshi, "My Journey to Christ."

a hospital, when my parents did not have a bed to sleep in as I did, they have been there. Even during the many blood transfusions and chemotherapies I receive, my mom and my dad, when he has been able to come, have always been there, sitting in the more uncomfortable chair, caring for me.

My friends—my roommate in particular—have had to deal with my uncertain health, react to any crisis, and be there by my side throughout my whole journey. It is through these sacrifices and more that I have come to see love personified, as people have sacrificed greatly for me, and I do not know how I can ever repay them.

Relationships are among some of the most important things in this life. After my battle with cancer, I came to realize how unimportant many things are, but how valuable relationships are. Your family, significant others, friends, and even those you interact with on a day-to-day basis all have deep meaning. Some make the mistake of placing their life's meaning on a person, as I did with my romantic relationships. But there are very few things more important than the relationships you will accumulate in your life. I can't pretend to know how to navigate them all, but if one starts with the groundwork of learning to view people with compassionate, deep love, then I think that at the very least is a good foundation to build upon.

While COVID may not have directly affected the outcome of my relationships, it has certainly put a spotlight on how much I need others. Oftentimes you don't realize how much something is really worth until you lose it. The season of isolation caused by COVID and my subsequent breakup showed me just how deeply my need to know and be known runs. It is this idea that drove me to my knees, realizing that other people would fail to fulfill this need and that I would need to look elsewhere to find true relational satisfaction.

BOOK TWO

Cancer

The Thirty-Day War

By the time January of 2021 rolled around, I was quite determined to put 2020 behind me. Who wasn't? Not only had it been a tough and challenging season because of COVID, but I was still battling loneliness because of my breakup, and my first semester of college had been primarily online. I was ready for a fresh start. I was hoping that my college classes would begin to be in person more and that my relationships would begin to deepen as a result. My roommate and I were involved in the same Bible study and it had turned out to be a brilliant community for me. Little did I know how much I was about to need them. As the 2020 year closed out, I wrote this as my end-of-the-year post:

> 2020 was definitely one of my harder years, and some of my struggles have been shared by the world and plenty aren't known by many but I choose to look back on it and see how much good it brought me. Good friends, old ones, generous family, and so much more. 2021 doesn't promise any better, but at least I know that through whatever happens I'll have joy through it all. Thank you to everyone who was a part of 2020 and to everyone who will be a part of 2021. God bless you all.

I wrote this post quite literally as the year changed over and I had a good start to 2021, spending time with some of my good friends. The next day I decided to begin the year with a water-only fast for forty-eight hours as I prayed for three specific people to know the Lord. The day after the fast, I went with my brother and grandparents to help my father move. Throughout the move I got tired extremely quickly and had to sit down often. My grandparents were actually outworking me, which I felt bad about. Once I had rest for a bit, I would feel fine again and would carry down a box or two before needing to rest again. It was odd to all of us, but because I had just ended my fast the day before we figured that I was probably just weak from that.

Back home I had begun to notice small red dots on my legs and arms. They weren't like pimples, though; they were not raised, it was just like someone had taken a small red pen and put dots all over my body. I first noticed these over Christmas break after hiking up a waterfall. It was a hike I had made several times before, but this time I lagged far behind my family. We figured that the slowness of my walk and the dots on my skin meant that I was out of shape and suffering from high blood pressure. So after Christmas break and into January, I had been making sure to walk and run at the very least a mile every day and I was more closely watching what I was eating. I had not been doing this my first semester of college, so I knew it should help.

Despite my newfound exercise routine, I noticed that I was actually getting worse. I would climb the stairs to my apartment, something I had done with ease for months, and be out of breath by the time I got to the top. This confused me since I thought I should be getting better, not worse, but I figured it was another sign that I was out of shape, and I was actually ashamed that I was out of breath, so I would always try to hide my breathing from my roommate so he wouldn't notice.

A week and a half after my dad moved, it was Thursday, January 14. I had a lot of Auburn's equivalent to "Dining Dollars," and so I was taking my mom to Auburn's campus for lunch. We both decided to take the approximately ten-minute walk from my apartment onto campus. It was a walk I had made nearly every day the previous semester to go to my only in-person class. However, it became very clear as we went along that I was not okay. I could not make it out of the parking lot before I had to stop walking to catch my breath. I had to stop another three or four times before we made it onto campus and by then I was in bad shape. I had felt at the beginning of the trip like I had done about a lap into a mile run. That is to say, the feeling of dread and fatigue that typically accompanies me when I run had taken over me. However, I come from a stubborn stock and so I put my unusual tiredness in the back of my mind and proceeded to push on.

I cannot begin to describe how strange it was for me to stop walking to catch my breath. You always go from running to walking when you're tired, but then you're always able to keep walking while you catch your breath. To have to come to a complete stop on the sidewalk while other people kept walking, and then when walking itself made me need to catch my breath, my red flags finally went up to a point where I could not ignore them any longer. When we finally got to where the food trucks were on campus, I was so tired that I nearly passed out. I have never passed out in my life but I very nearly did then. My vision was filled with black spots, I was about to throw up, and had I not leaned my head back and regulated my breathing

I am certain that I would have passed out then and there. After I sat down for a bit and got back under control, I still felt too exhausted to even eat, so my mom ate as we discussed that it was probably time for me to get tested for COVID. It made sense to the both of us that my shortness of breath would be caused by the global pandemic. I called out of my extended day job, which was the first time I had ever done that, and went to get a COVID test the next day. I did a same-day test, and to my surprise the result came back negative.

My mom tried to get me into a doctor's office that day once my test came back negative, but we were not able to get into one until Saturday morning. That night my mom, one of her lifelong friends, and I went to grab dinner at our favorite steak restaurant. My mom's friend remarked that my coloring was off, and we spent most of the night debating what we thought I might have had. The general ideas that were being thrown out were something to do with diabetes or possibly a heart issue, because, along with my shortness of breath, my heart rate was beginning to be in the 110–115-beats-per-minute range even when I was lying in bed.

The next morning, my mom and I went to visit Auburn Pediatric and Adult Medicine, where they were holding a walk-in clinic over the weekend. There they performed an EKG test and saw that my heart was tachycardic. Tachycardia is the medical term for a heart rate over 100 beats per minute (bpm). This can be caused by a variety of reasons. It was concerning for me because it was exceeding 100 bpm while I was at rest. I was seeing my primary care physician on that day, and he decided to run more extensive blood work than just the initial finger prick tests.

My mom and I sat in the room laughing at a *Babylon Bee* article when my primary care physician walked in, and we could tell by looking at his face that something was very wrong. He proceeded to read us the numbers from my bloodwork and highlighted that my red blood cells were extremely low. In fact, all of my numbers were extremely low except for one: my white blood cells. My white blood cell count was in the 40,000 range. They normally do not exceed 11,000. My primary care physician did not diagnose me, but my mom and I both knew what those numbers meant. She started crying and we were told to not leave the doctor's office until he had secured us a room at the University of Alabama in Birmingham Hospital for that day. My mom called a close friend, who came immediately and sat with us, and for about the next thirty minutes we sat there and called my father and told him the news. Soon the doctor told us that he had secured a room for me and I was to go home, pack, and leave for Birmingham as soon as possible.

This was a lot to take in very quickly, to realize you are in a serious enough condition to need to go to the top hospital in the state. Beforehand we thought that at the worst I would need to go to East Alabama Medical Center, our local hospital, but we did not even think that was a realistic possibility. It was so little on our minds that beforehand we had joked about it, but we were not joking anymore.

I was told to pack and prepare for a four-to-five day stay and so I drove back to my apartment and my mom to her house and I quickly scrambled to pack my suitcase. My roommate was busy that day but he helped me pack a little before he had to leave. I told him that it was possible I had leukemia, and that I would be gone for a few days. His eyes widened at the thought of me being gone for so long. After we had packed everything, he left and one of the members of our Bible study was kind enough to bring me some lunch.

Soon after, my mom and I began the two-hour drive to Birmingham, Alabama. It is quite hard to put a finger on the emotions I experienced during that drive. I think I was partially in shock, but I was also peaceful. In a crisis I am never one to flip out; I just buckle down and do what needs to be done to resolve the situation. We made several phone calls along the way, including one to my former pediatrician, who was able to comfort my mom better than anyone else. That car ride was the first time in my life I had ever contemplated what death might truly look like for me. I was also diving headfirst into the unknown. I had no idea about the world of cancer. I knew it was bad, of course, and that it caused people tremendous suffering, but I had no idea what that actually looked like or what I was about to experience.

We arrived in Birmingham around four thirty in the afternoon, where we met up with my dad, who had come about an hour and a half away. From there we were temperature scanned, and my parents walked (I got the luxurious wheelchair treatment) over to the Women's and Infants Center, or WIC. We went up to the eighth floor and I was shown into my room. I proceeded to have my vitals checked and then what felt like the entire nursing staff came in to help admit me. There were six to ten nurses in the room because it was right about time for shift change, so they were helping my nurse out. However, for me it had been a long day and seeing all of those nurses in there certainly panicked me. It reinforced the seriousness of the situation, but they reassured me that their high numbers did not correlate to me being in a critical state at that time.

I had blood drawn from both arms and an IV placed in both as well. I was COVID tested once again, because the WIC was the only building at UAB that was being kept COVID-free at all times. As they were placing the IVs, they needed to use vein finders and ultrasound to get good veins, and both of those machines were fascinating. This moment gave our family a simple break from the chaos as we watched those two machines do their work.

During this hectic time, I also remember, rather embarrassingly, that I denied clergy. One of the questions they ask as they check you in is whether or not you're religious and, if you are, whether you'd like a member of the clergy to see you. To the first I responded yes, but when they asked the second, I blurted out no. You see, my father used to be a pastor and my mother was a social worker in hospice for a very long time, so in that moment all my mind could think about was a correlation between clergy seeing people and them passing away, so in a split second I denied clergy. I guess I was thinking that denial somehow would help me to not die. I laugh thinking back on that situation, but at the moment I was quite scared of clergy.

As the night went on, my mother, father, and I sat in the room and talked. I will admit I cannot remember what all we talked about. The next thing I recall was the on-call doctor entering my room around eleven o'clock with the official diagnosis. It was leukemia. My mother and I had been expecting this result, so, while it was certainly hard to hear for the two of us, it was a little harder on my father.

By the time I got into the hospital, my white blood cell count had gone from 40,000 to 54,000. For reference, once your white blood cells hit 100,000 it becomes extremely hard to treat. I also had anemia due to the low count of oxygen-carrying cells in my blood. So, in about thirteen hours I went from having no outstanding previous medical history to having cancer. The next week would become one of the more challenging weeks as I got tests such as x-rays, blood transfusions, massive amounts of new information thrown at me, and was told that I would need to begin chemotherapy as soon as possible in order to have a chance at survival.

Normally, I would have been able to begin operations on Monday, but that was Martin Luther King Jr. Day and so many of the regular team was going to be out. You see, before chemotherapy could begin, they needed to figure out which type of leukemia it was. There are four main types: acute myeloid (or myelogenous) leukemia (AML), chronic myeloid (or myelogenous) leukemia (CML), acute lymphocytic (or lymphoblastic) leukemia (ALL), and chronic lymphocytic leukemia (CLL). Because of the fast rate of growth, the doctors believed I had one of the acute leukemias, and of those two they were thinking, and I was hoping, that it was ALL. ALL is found more often in younger people. To figure out the type of leukemia, my doctor and her team had to take an extensive look at my bloodwork as well as do a bone marrow biopsy for more specifics. I also needed what is called a PICC line, which is a tube that runs from the arm to my heart, allowing the doctors and nurses to administer chemo drugs, blood transfusions, or just regular fluids without having to stick me with an IV each time. Normally I would have gotten this tube Monday, but because of the holiday I did not get it until Tuesday.

On Tuesday I was told that the doctors would be taking a look at my bloodwork to determine the type of leukemia, with a bone marrow biopsy planned for Wednesday. On Wednesday the doctors came in and told me that it was actually AML, which was very hard for me to hear. AML is associated with significantly lower outcomes as compared to ALL. Immediately after the diagnosis, we did a bone marrow biopsy, which was a miserable experience for me. I had asked to take a quick walk before we began because not only did I not know what to expect from the biopsy, but I was devastated by the diagnosis. I was so emotional that the anti-anxiety medicine they gave me beforehand had little effect on me.

I have only cried three times throughout this whole ordeal. Once it was because I realized that it was a possibility that I might die, and I did not want that to happen in the hospital. I did not want to have suddenly gone up to UAB and to have never had the chance to say an in-person goodbye to my friends and family. The second time was during the biopsy, because I was so emotional about my diagnosis, and the third was when people came to give me a surprise visit in the hospital. But I want to go back to the second time I cried, when I was receiving my first biopsy.

When doing a biopsy, your skin and the surface of your bone are numbed, then a needle is inserted into the bone and samples are extracted. Then they chip off a piece of your bone about the size of the tip of a pen. The pain begins once the needle enters your bone, because they cannot numb that area of the body. It is also painful as they draw the marrow out. Even though the surface of the bone is numb, I cannot understate how weird it is to feel something tapping into the back of your hip bone. It is the most unnatural thing I think I have ever felt. There is no pain when they chip the bone off because it is numbed, but it still feels incredibly uncomfortable.

After the biopsy, I laid in bed for a bit before going for a walk. Even though I was sore, the doctors always said that the way you could help yourself was by walking, and so I did. The difficult thing to wrestle with during this time was the fact that there was nothing I could do to determine the outcome of my life. I asked the doctors repeatedly if there was anything I could do to help the chemo fight off the cancer, but the answer was always, "really no." Keeping my emotions positive and going for walks was something they recommended, but there was nothing I could do that would truly help. The next step was to begin my chemotherapy on that same day, January 20.

The plan was for me to receive two kinds of drugs: cytarabine and idarubicin. The cytarabine I would get twenty-four hours a day for a week, while the much harsher idarubicin would be administered on the first three days. The purpose of the chemotherapy drugs is to attack rapidly producing cells. However, they do not have the power to tell the difference between rapidly growing cancer cells and quickly growing normal cells. That is why you lose your hair and may have certain side effects. Several days into my chemotherapy, the doctors came back with the news that I had a gene called inversion 16. Simply put, this meant that they could give me a third drug known as Mylotarg, which would specifically target the leukemia cells with that genetic change. They gave me the Mylotarg one day over the course of that week.

People have often asked me what it is like to have chemo, and honestly while it is going in it doesn't feel like anything. In the movies we often see chemo and radiation together, but I did not have any radiation. The chemotherapy I got was all through my PICC line, and so it went into me like any other fluid would have. For the week that I was getting the chemo, I was attached through my PICC line to the machine that was pumping it into my body. That meant that whenever I stood up to go to the bathroom, as you do a lot with as many fluids as they give you, or to take a walk, I had to bring the machine with me. I wore slippers anytime I got up from the bed so as to not touch the floor that the nurses, who went from room to room, also walked on. I could look out the window in my room and I could walk around the halls for a bit, but I could never leave the floor.

The ability to walk was a great freedom for me as it allowed me to escape the four walls of my room, but it never lasted very long as I was quickly tired. Occasionally other patients would be out walking as well. I remember one lady in particular, who had to have been in her fifties or sixties, but she was full of energy and would even lap me. There were two windows in these halls that became particularly important to me. One allowed me to overlook the front courtyard of the WIC and see people who came to visit me. The other allowed me to look out and see UAB Children's and several parking lots and restaurants below. There is not much to look out at, but when it is your only view of the outside world, it becomes very important to you.

During this first week, I was attached to the machine, like I said, except for about twenty minutes. Around six or seven o'clock the nurse would come and disconnect me from the pump while chemo was being changed from one to another. This allowed me some time to take a shower, but also to be free. In fact, on nights when I was particularly tired of being tethered, I would walk around the room saying, "I'm free." I probably sounded like Gollum from *Lord of the Rings* to all who listened. I will also note that you cannot just take a shower while you are in the hospital. For one, you have an external line that is going straight to your heart that has to be capped and covered with a plastic sleeve that has elastic on both sides. This sleeve covered my arm from my wrist to my right bicep in order to keep my PICC line from getting wet. Then you are always trying to not step on the floor, so I would have to try to disrobe while never putting my feet anywhere but on the towels we had laid on the floor. Now, the showers there were always nice and hot, and for that I was always very appreciative, but I couldn't enjoy it for long because I had to get hooked back up quickly. When I was finished, I had to do my tightrope act once again to get dressed and I had to use special wipes to clean the part of my arm that had been covered up by the plastic sleeve. After my showers I would call my nurse back, who would hook me up to my chemo.

While it was, in a way, crazy to think that I had started chemo less than a week after I had even gone to the doctor, there was a certain peace once it had started. You do not know if it will work; you have to wait for that. But the effects of the chemo have not set in and so you're left feeling quite well. In fact, I felt better that first week of chemo then I had the week prior because I finally had blood that was closer to normal. Once I was unhooked from chemo the next week, I had even more freedom than I had felt was possible. I was able to go to the bathroom without dragging a machine with me, although out of habit I sometimes accidentally took it in there even though I was unattached. I cannot tell you how freeing it is to no longer be attached to a machine. I still had to be attached sometimes to receive fluids or medication, but I did not have to be hooked up all of the time, and that was freeing.

About a week after starting chemo, the side effects began to set in. I was fortunate to only vomit twice. The nurses and doctors kept me well regulated with medicine to prevent nausea. I did begin to experience a lot of tiredness. I slept for most of the day, and I was very lethargic. At its worst, I did not even have the energy to turn on the TV to watch shows, or my tablet to play games and FaceTime people. On those days, the most I could do was respond to texts and take a shower. We also made sure that I went on at least two walks around the unit a day, no matter how tired I was. I was always very conflicted about my walks and showers because often I felt too tired to do them, but they were also my only escape from the hospital bed, so I wanted to take them. Sometimes I would go sit in the chairs with either my mom or dad just to get out of the bed. However, there were days when I was too tired to even do that. My dad had brought a dartboard and Battleship, so we played those occasionally. However, I cannot overstate just how tired I was. Prior to cancer, after a day or two of doing nothing I would normally at least find myself something to do. But I did not while I was in the hospital. I was content to lay there for days on end because I was too tired to do much else.

Due to COVID regulations at the hospital, my mom and dad were not allowed to stay with me at the same time and I was not allowed any other visitors, so they rotated in and out throughout the course of my stay. Each time they came was exciting for me because each would always bring some new letters or gifts that very generous people had sent me, and it always made my day. However, I did miss seeing people. My parents were brilliant and I was able to hang out with them over that month all day and all night without ever once having a conflict. But to see anyone else, I had to either call or FaceTime, or if they were kind enough to drive up to Birmingham to see me, they would stand in the courtyard and wave up to me in the window while we talked over the phone. That was one of the most painful things for me: to sit there and see someone who had spent about four hours driving come so close, but still be eight stories away with a glass window between me and them. To not be able to see them in person nor to have any way to thank them for their kindness was very hard for me. It made me more determined to leave no matter what so I could hug those people and see them face to face. But I am very thankful for all of those who came; it is part of what kept me going.

As the second week wound on, I was closing in on day fourteen since chemotherapy started. That would be the day of my second bone marrow biopsy, when we would find out whether or not the chemo had worked. Throughout the first two weeks, and really throughout my entire time in the hospital, people were always sending me encouraging and touching notes, so much so that we were taping them up on the cabinets in my room and we were running out of space. I looked at them night and day—and yes, I was awake for a large part of the night. While in the hospital, my regular sleeping hours went out of the door. Vitals are checked every three hours, so you never really have the opportunity to sleep for an extended time before you are woken up again. That is also another reason why I slept often during the day. You sleep whenever you can. My parents would sleep on the couch they had in the room as the back cushion could fold down to make a reasonably nice bed. My mom says she always looked out and saw the Vulcan, a statue in Birmingham, and it became a symbol of hope to her.

You might wonder how my parents coped through all of this experience, but I do not know that I could answer fully. I know they both were in a sort of crisis mode, but they also had a certain air of peace about them. Neither of them ever acted in a distressed manner, at least in my presence, although my dad did get woken up from a nap by someone coming in the room and he yelled in surprise as he spun up from the couch, which I found quite funny. What was difficult for them was that they could not touch me. Because they were going from the outside world into my room and I had absolutely no immune system, giving me a hug, holding my hand, or any other form of comforting touch from parent to child was out of the picture. This was the situation we were in as we approached day fourteen.

During these few weeks, the doctors had to run an ultrasound on my liver. They had noticed that it was becoming fatty and wanted to find out why. When I got my ultrasound, it took approximately ten minutes, but I was stuck in a separate wing for two hours because they were short-staffed in transportation. My mom was more upset about it than anything, as she had no way to contact me to find out what was going on. Eventually, the doctors ruled that there was not a problem as long as it was stabilized. They also noticed that my blood sugar was high. This was caused by the steroids that I had been given prior to chemotherapy. I was essentially told that I should not eat certain foods because of my blood sugar, but that because of my chemo I should try to eat anything I could, so they would just monitor it with insulin.

You had to be very careful of what you touched in the hospital. For example, I had to make sure that after I used the bathroom I did not touch anything else, even by accident, until I had washed my hands. I tried to never touch the floor with my feet, and I was always careful to try to never touch my face with my hands. If someone did touch the floor, or something from outside of the room, we made sure they and anything they touched were washed before coming near me. If anything fell on the floor, it had to be wiped with Lysol before I could touch it again. This is because I could have gotten an infection very easily. In fact, I was so immunocompromised that the two infections I would later get didn't originate from someone bringing them in, but rather from my own body. I was not able to fight off the normal bacteria that exists inside of us on a regular basis. These are just a few of the several small problems that can pop up while you are in the hospital.

So finally day fourteen came and I got my bone marrow biopsy. Over the next few days, while I was waiting, I emailed a pastor, and I think that email describes my mindset at the time better than I can now.

> It is no small task to have to face the real potential of your own mortality at any time, much less when you are nineteen and still in college. I have had to learn to give all pieces of my future, my career, my want to get married, to have a family, completely to God because I do not know if those are things I will get to experience.
>
>   I like to have control. But I have none moving forward other than how I impact others toward Christ. I find out today if the chemotherapy has worked and that will determine if I can go home or if I'll need more. I am at peace with whichever comes

my way. There are two stories that come to mind, of the leper and of Shadrach, Meshach, and Abednego. Like the leper, and many others who Jesus healed, I have been telling the Lord that I know he can heal me if He is willing, and have been asking for healing. But also like Shadrach, Meshach, and Abednego I say that even if He does not save me from this my hope is still rested in Him.

That day the results from my biopsy came back: there was no evidence of cancer in the biopsy. My family and I truly rejoiced as now we could relax with the knowledge that soon I would be able to return home. From there I had to wait for my immune system to return to a place where I would be able to be out in public without high risk of infection.

During the second week, when my chemo symptoms were the worst, I began to experience nausea, but it was strangely caused by a hyperactive sense of smell. I have never been able to smell better than I could during that week and I can promise you that super-smell will never be on my wish list. My dad bought Moe's Southwest for dinner one night, and I was able to tell which bag had the chips, which one had the beef bowl, and which one had the steak quesadilla just by smelling through the bag. Even the water and the cabinet drawers had an individual, intense smell to me. I was unable to eat much in the hospital. It was not a lack of appetite at first, but rather certain foods made me nauseous. Soon, though, my ability to eat did diminish. I was hungry and felt like I could eat a horse, but once I started eating I became full very quickly. There were several weeks where I was not able to finish half of a hamburger.

When it came to food, I was determined early on to eat as much hospital food as possible, because it was included in my stay. I would call as soon as I woke up and I found that the breakfast I could eat the most consistently was a sausage patty, a biscuit, a hard-boiled egg (much to the disdain of my parents, who were happy on the days I chose scrambled), yogurt, and grits. I always had various pills, which I have never been good at swallowing, but I learned quickly, so I would take those with each meal as well. The only time I did not get this breakfast was my second-to-last day in the hospital, when I had Waffle House. For lunch I would eat a light ham sandwich, or something similar, and I would order a heavier dinner of a cheeseburger, soup, fish, or whatever was on the menu that night. I would also get either a brownie or ice cream for dessert and that was my favorite part. However, as time went on, especially in the second week, when it was hard to find something more than Cheez-Its and goldfish crackers that I could stomach, we moved away from hospital food. The menu was always the same every week and we figured that variety would help keep nausea away, and it did. So for lunch and dinner my parents would be gracious enough to walk to one of the nearby restaurants or the grill downstairs and get me some food. This is the way we did meals through the remainder of the hospital stay.

Once we knew that I would be going home when my immune system had been restored, we expected to be going back after about a week. However, those low immune system numbers would come back to haunt me. I ended up getting two infections over my last two weeks in the hospital, which made life much harder. You see, each time you get a fever in the hospital, you have to get stuck in both arms to have blood drawn so they can see if you have an infection. I hated this in particular because they rarely got blood from my left arm, so I ended up getting stuck four or five times on some occasions. When I did get an infection, my body would grew feverish because that was the only natural response it had. This caused many miserable nights where I had to place ice packs all over my body with no covers on to try to break my fever. There was one occasion where I needed a blood transfusion but they could not give it to me because I had a fever that hadn't broken for almost two days.

Once the infections had cleared, I had to spend about another week in the hospital, even though I felt fine, and I was restless the whole time. It was around day twenty-one that I finally lost my hair. We were told it would probably fall out between day ten and day fourteen, so when we hit day twenty and it had not come out, we thought that I was going to hold onto it. My desire, like many others, I'm told, was to wait and see if it would actually all come out. Waiting was a mistake. It did come out. One of the most uncomfortable feelings in the world is that of laying in your hair. I had a lot of it, so it got everywhere. It was all over the pillows, all over the floor, and in the shower, and it was miserable. When I finally shaved my head, I was not traumatized by it; I just wanted it all gone so I could have some peace.

During that time, I was also quarantined in my room for ten days because of my infections, and that was very hard. I was only able to pace around my room, but I was feeling better than I had my entire stay, so when they finally announced that I would get to leave soon, I was more than ecstatic. I was cleared to go but, because it was the weekend and the pharmacy with my medicine was closed, I had to wait until Monday. On Monday morning the nurse practitioner informed us that they might hold me to watch my liver numbers, and for the first time in my entire stay I began to have true frustration. I had made it through the diagnosis, chemotherapy, and infections and had kept a good head on throughout. But when I had been told all weekend that I would be going home and was then told on the day of that I night not, I finally broke. By "broke" I mean that I stood by the window banging my head and saying "Let me out" for quite some time, and my mom thought that I had finally lost it.

Eventually, my doctor came in and told me that they would go ahead with discharging me. So, throughout the day we finished packing what had been our hotel room for a month, my PICC line was pulled, and I was wheeled out to the car. It was my first time being off the hospital floor in thirty days. It was the day after Valentine's Day, and my mom and I decided to stop by the Cheesecake Factory to celebrate. I will never forget the feeling of riding out of the parking garage, being out in the open, and experiencing the wind and weather again. I spent the ride home talking about how nice it was just to be able to ride.

Since then, I have spent three months going back to UAB. I first had to get a third bone marrow biopsy to see if any new leukemia cells were being made. Amazingly, there were not any and the malfunctioned gene that had caused my leukemia in the first place was not growing back in the new bone marrow. However, if we did no more chemo, the likelihood of cancer coming back was almost certain because there might have still been one or two leukemia cells in my body, which would not be a problem at first, but as time went on it would grow into more. That is why I have gone back for follow-up chemotherapy.

I get what is called HIDAC. It is the cytarabine I received initially but in a higher dose. My mom and I drive up to Birmingham on Monday nights and will often go and see a movie at a very nice local theater that night. Then we meet with my doctor on Tuesday morning and begin chemo that night. I have to go early in the morning to get lab work done, and an IV has to be placed into my arm. If I am lucky, as we were on the second trip, the IV will work in my forearm. Otherwise, it usually goes into my right elbow, and so I have to keep my arm straight all week, including at night.

Each day we wake up around five thirty, leave the hotel, run by Dunkin' for my mom to get her coffee, and then we go and I get lab work done. I have to get labs done every day. Then we do morning chemo, which usually lasts until about ten thirty to eleven. After that, we are free to run around the city or go to our hotel and take a nap before returning around five thirty to six for the night chemo, which usually lasts until about nine. From there, we will go back to the hotel and go straight to bed, to do it again the next day. This is always a hard week for my mom and me due to the lack of sleep. Each time I go back, the chemo also takes a harder toll on me. I become tired more quickly, my skin breaks out more, and I tend to not recover as fast in the weeks that follow. But the hardships do not matter. I am very thankful to not be in the hospital right now. I get to enjoy the pleasures of being out in the world every day. I have to do lab work twice a week and often I need blood transfusions in the weeks in between chemo, but I am happy for the work the chemo is doing in my body.

As I write this, I will return in about a month for my fourth bone marrow biopsy. This one will tell us whether I need three or four rounds of chemo. Then either I will do one more round of follow-up chemo or I will be done, which would be amazing. I do hope that it will be three, as each round of chemo hits me harder, but I also realize how rare and fortunate that would be. In fact, I have experienced worse symptoms from the chemotherapy than I did from leukemia. When I was diagnosed with leukemia, my hemoglobin (which distributes oxygen in the body) was around six and a half. Under chemo, it has gotten into the fives, while it should normally be sixteen. My platelets (the blood particles that stop bleeding) were at seven with leukemia but have gotten to as low as four under chemo, whereas they should be 150 or higher. But all of this is necessary to keep the leukemia away. As I write this all down, I realize there are certainly some things I have left out accidentally. It is a lot to have changed in just a few short months and to condense it to these few pages is crazy. But now you know my story thus far from my perspective. This has been my cancer experience.

Death on the Doorstep

Death is not a topic very many people like to discuss. We like to ignore the finality of life as much as possible, but I, now more than ever, believe that people should face this fear and would do well to remember the reality of death. Growing up, I had never seriously considered my mortality. Very few youths do. I have had many people in my life who have been very close and then suddenly left, but I never had someone leave in the permanence that is death. Up until this point, all of my grandparents and one great-grandparent have been fortunate to have long lives.

When you are young, you always think that death is far away. When you picture your life, you think about making it to college, then perhaps getting married and finding a big-boy/girl job, raising a family, working for a few decades while raising said family, and then eventually retiring and doing what you love. Then maybe you would start thinking about death. This was at least how I thought about my own life. Even when you hear about the occasional exception, the child killed in a car accident, for example, you always are sad but you never think that it could apply to you. Mortality is just not something you consider to be an actual possibility.

On January 16, when my mother and I were driving up to Birmingham, soon to find out I had leukemia, I seriously contemplated death for the first time. Now, when somebody does, I think most people's first instinct to say something along the lines of, "Now put that thought out of your mind and focus on the positive," but I could not. For the first time in my life, I was faced with a very real chance that I might die, and I was not concerned with giving myself false hope. However, I think that even then I did not fully realize the gravity of the situation. The reality was that the cancer I had was attacking extremely fast. The doctors told me that I probably had no cancer on Thanksgiving of 2020, and had I not received medical treatment I would probably not have lived through January of 2021. If you remember that ever-important white blood cell count, it took only twelve hours for my white blood cells to grow from 40,000 to 54,000. At around the 100,000 mark it becomes extremely difficult to treat. The reality was that I was in real jeopardy, and while I may not have known how much so at the time, I did realize that death was a possibility and that it would not be unrealistic for me to consider it.

Despite the situation, I was not scared as some would expect. Most of my thoughts revolved around what the experience would be like. I wondered what dying would even feel like. As the first week in the hospital came and went, I did not receive any word as to the likelihood of my survival. If you remember, the doctors were hoping that I had ALL. ALL is associated with better survival outcomes and is often found in younger patients. This is why it was particularly devastating for me when the doctors informed me that the diagnosis was AML, which is rare to find in someone so young. Still, they said that the goal was to achieve a complete cure, so on with chemo we went. However, despite my asking multiple times, there was ultimately nothing I could do to help the chemo work or not. All I could do was let the chemo go into me and pray for healing.

There was an agonizing two weeks where we were essentially in limbo, wondering if the chemo would work or not. If it had not, we would have moved on to another round of harsh chemo along with possibly a bone marrow transplant, but my survival chances would have dropped significantly. Thankfully the chemo did its job, but for two weeks I had to consider that I did not know how long I would survive. Even now, even though I have been blessed with as good a healing as I think I could have, I look to the future with uncertainty.

Facing death opened my eyes to a lot that I had previously ignored and fired up a lot of new perspectives. The first and foremost thing was that it caused me to solidify my relationship with God. I had been a Christian long before I was diagnosed, so it is not like I waited until my deathbed to get right with God. The possibility of coming face to face with him soon was odd to consider but, honestly, I'd be lying if said that didn't fill me with some excitement. To be in the presence of a being that is pure love, goodness, power, and might and to peer beyond the curtain of life fascinated me. It also caused me to look at my whole life as a big picture and that caused me to see just how fragile life is as well as what the important things are in life.

I do not think dying scared me personally. I knew that with death would come an end to my suffering, and if I was right about how I see the world and if my relationship with God was true, then every tear would be wiped away and my new life would only be beginning.[2]

---

2. See Revelation 21:4.

If I was wrong, then that was simply just it for me and there was no real fear there. What did cause me trouble was thinking about all the people whom I would be causing pain. Family and friends would feel my absence, plus I did not want to die without having said goodbye. I think the act of having to say goodbye would have been difficult for me. But, in a way, I would have been thankful and will be if it is cancer that takes me out versus, say, a sudden car wreck. At least with cancer you have the time to say good-bye and straighten things out, and that is at the very least something I would be happy to have the chance to do.

While ultimately I have been healed so far, I think it is important to remember just how close death really can be. Life goes a lot quicker than it feels as you are going about your day-to-day activities. I am an advocate for living in the present, as I have been guilty in the past of always looking off to the future, but someday, not that far off in the future, we will all face our death. I think it is good to keep this in mind. It changes how you interact with people, affects your actions on a day-to-day basis, and forces you to truly take a look at the meaningful questions about life. A friend recently asked me if I am ever scared by looking back and realizing how close I was to death, and the answer is no. It caused me to look at the meaning of life, but I think it was a good thing that I faced those questions and I have a much better and more realistic outlook on my life and existence after my time in the hospital. Ultimately death will find all of us, and it might serve us better to not ignore that reality, but rather to embrace and prepare for it while we still have the time that is given to us.

Impact

I think that one of the most humbling things that happened while I was in the hospital was the outreach and support I received from so many people from so many different walks of life. Throughout my stay in the hospital and even after, I have continued to see the best of humanity. At first, it was in the calls and texts once we announced my diagnosis publicly. I had people who I had not spoken to for years contacting me and showing their support. Then letters started pouring in from friends, family, my fellow theater students, my extended-day kids, my high school teachers, and my Bible study, all of them touching me. The words varied, some offering support if I needed anything, some saying they were sorry that I was going through this experience, some saying how much I had meant to them, and some offering advice. I took it all in with gratitude and I very suddenly began to realize just how many people I had crossed paths with in life. This is not to toot my own horn; I don't consider myself to be popular, so it was quite a shock for me to see just how many people I had touched. It also humbled me, because I knew, if I were honest, that I had not treated every interaction with people in the loving kind way that I am called to.

As time moved on, people began to donate to a GoFundMe that would help with our initial cost of treatment. People were extremely generous, and what I found through that was that many of my former classmates as well as fellow college students who did not have much in the way of money often made the largest donations. People also sent in various things, whether it be snacks, ChapStick, flavors for water, or things to do to preoccupy my mind. The more that people donated, the more humbled I felt. There was no way that I could repay the generosity that was being shown to me. I still cannot. I was being shown pure human kindness, and for that I am ever grateful. About a month after I left the hospital, I wrote a thank you note that sums up my thanks accurately:

Since my leukemia diagnosis I have been met with support that I could not have imagined and I am both humbled and speechless as to how to thank those of you who have helped my family and me.

I have seen such an outpouring of generosity, be it in the form of meals, prayers, texts, calls, donations, cards, or just spending time with me- it has all touched my heart.

I do not know what the future holds, but I can say that I sit now in a place of joy and I am content. I have seen a great outpouring of love and care and I thank you all for that. Please continue to do so if you are able.

After I left the hospital, people continued to be generous to both my family and me, giving us gift cards and making meals for us so that for months afterward we were able to stay fed. I don't think my mom or I had to buy groceries for months, and that was all because of the tremendous support of others. Not only does it make you realize just how great humanity can be when we all demonstrate kindness and selflessness, but it humbles you to realize just how impactful each interaction you have can be. I again had people reaching out to me that told me how important my kindness had been to them in just our small interactions. But I also cringe because I realize that I have had interactions where I did the opposite, and that makes me very sad. The people who sent in everything, who drove to visit me, who called and texted to keep my spirits alive, and especially those who have spent time with me in the months following my hospital stay will never realize how important their actions were and how they sustained me through those hard times.

The importance of prayer is also something I do not overlook. During the days the doctors said I would be feeling my worst, I felt my best, even asking my nurse, "Is it okay for me to be feeling this good?" I am convinced that the healing I have experienced has been in part due to the many advocates on my behalf, and I am thankful for having so many countless people who have prayed for me. There was no shortage of messages that I received where people offered to pray for me, but even more moving were the churches all the way from Tennessee to Florida who gathered to pray for me, and that moved me. It showed me the undeserved care that complete strangers had on my behalf and that truly meant the world to me. The care that everyone showed me during the month in the hospital conveyed the clear message of love and showed just how loving humanity can be at its best.

The month in the hospital taught me not only that other people have had a profound impact on my life, but, I realize now, just how much impact mine has had on others, and moving forward I have stopped taking my day-to-day interactions so lightly and realize that sometimes it is the simple kind gesture, selfless giving, or spending time with another person that truly makes an impact.

The Lilies of the Field

If there is one thing that cancer has changed about me, it is my perspective on life itself. Very quickly I realized just how wrong my perspective had been and how much I had cared about trivial things. If you remember back to the very beginning of this book, I complained about a certain theater role that I did not get. At the moment, I was horribly devastated because I did not get my desired role. During COVID, I was devastated because of all the events I had lost. I was extremely devastated when I lost my relationship. Oftentimes it would not have even taken heavy life situations to wreck me. Looking back, I realize just how much being late for work or school, rushing to turn in an assignment, a bad hair day, car problems, my phone not working, a disagreement with a friend or family member, and so much more could take a simple, normal day and make it worse. But as I lay there in the hospital, staring at what may have been the end of my life, not a single thought was devoted to any of those things. I was not worried about my roles in shows, or past stressful deadlines, or what I was going to wear, or if the food I was able to eat was going to be up to my standards, or if the post somebody made was annoying. No, I was not worried about any of these things. Instead, I was worried about my relationships, how I had impacted others, and what I had done with my life.

As I lay there, I realized that I had spent so much of my time always staring forward toward the future, causing me to miss out on a lot of the beauties of the present. Some of you reading this won't struggle with that; in fact, some of you may realize you need to pay more attention to the future. For me, though, it was an eye-opening revelation that I had very nearly wasted my life striving for my plan for the future, a future that I very nearly did not have and one I am still not guaranteed. Here I was working through childhood to get to middle school, and middle school to get to high school, and high school to get to college, and the purpose of college was to land a job, and the purpose of the job would be to make it to retirement, and the purpose of retirement would be to spend time with family before I go to heaven, which was the purpose of my life to make it there. I was always doing things with an eye on the future, but in doing so I missed out on enjoying where I was in life at the moment.

I realized almost too late that there would be no point in striving for my dream job if my life was going to end at nineteen. If I had sacrificed the present but never got the reward (the job, house, family, etc), all of my efforts would have been in vain. Now, I am not saying to swing the pendulum to the other side and ignore the future, because that is dangerous as well. There is a healthy way to balance seeing your future and still being in the present. If you live each day with a general outline of the future but always remain attentive and thankful for the small things that you are given in a day, then I think you and I have set a good foundation.

You see, that's what you miss when you pay attention to only the future. When I am striving to make it to that show two weeks from now and just hurrying through my days until I get there, I miss out on the fact that I am able to eat today or that I have a good conversation with a friend. Perhaps I don't take the time to slow down and go beyond the surface level with my friend because I am too much in a rush. I am certainly guilty of that. In the past, I have ended deep conversations abruptly because I had another minor appointment to go to, but I didn't care that it was minor, only that it was a meeting I had to make. I do not do that anymore.

I remember that while I was in the hospital my grandmother called and she was rambling, and my dad was getting annoyed by how long she was going on, but I remember that while I too would have been annoyed in the past, I was not anymore. I was soaking in every word because now that I truly felt that time was scarce, and every word she was saying to me had value. That is ultimately what much of this boils down to. What is the true value of things, and where are our priorities?

What I also learned is that several Bible verses became very real to me. Even if you do not believe in the Bible, I think the truths can still apply to you. The first thing that became very real to me is that our life here on Earth is merely a mist, here one day and gone the next as described in James 4:14. I have not realized until now what that means because, again, as a youth you feel that you have decades left to live the life you imagine for yourself. However, that is just not true. The truth is that your time may be limited to your youth, but even if you have all the decades you imagine for yourself, it is not that long in the grand scheme of life. It is not that long ago that my parents were my age, and though it is just a bit farther back, the reality is that my grandparents, though they have all lived long and full lives, were young just a few short years ago. Life tends to move much quicker than we realize, and before we know it, it is gone. So it is important to not be scared of that fact, because you cannot do anything about death, but rather to go ahead and embrace it by living your life now without procrastination, without waiting until later to sort out the meaningful questions of life or to repair that broken relationship.

I am not advocating for the frivolous lifestyle of YOLO (you only live once) culture, which sacrifices the future for hedonism in order to "live your best life now." Rather, I believe, now more than ever, that our time here is a precious gift. You would (hopefully) not take a gift and waste it immediately, but rather you would treat it well and make it useful for as long as you could. Another thing that I have seen through all of this is just how faithful God is to provide. In Matthew 6:26–34 Jesus talks about how God provides for the birds and clothes the lilies, and so God will do even more so for you. Now some would look at my suffering and question how God has provided for me. However, I have never seen God provide more than now. Whether it is in food, finances, gifts, or more, I have received more through this time than I even know what to do with. Through people, he has given and given abundantly.

I also want to note that there is a second part to that passage, where God not only says he will provide, but because he provides it is not for us to worry. I have read that passage my whole life, but it never really sunk in until I had to live it out. You see, often we worry about what kind of food would be best or we worry if the clothes we wear will be liked by others, or if our hair looks good or not. I am not saying that we shouldn't care about these things, but I have been unable to eat before. I've experienced when the clothes I wore didn't matter, and I still don't have hair so I know I won't be impressing anybody with that soon. You see, the issue is not that we care about those things, but rather that we often care too much about things we have no business worrying about. With this shift in my thinking of what materialistically matters, I began to realize what existentially matters.

Pursuing Permanence

By far, one of the biggest things that has changed because of my journey through cancer has been my view of what is meaningful in life and subsequently what my purpose is. My mother and I have talked extensively about how even the very fabric of our conversations with others has changed. It quite honestly has become a lot more difficult to hear people complain about their food or their clothes or their hair on a particular day after I have gone through cancer, because I realize that those kinds of things just don't matter. The stark reality that became very apparent to me was how much I used to care about things that didn't matter at all. When I was in the hospital, it didn't matter what I ate as long as I was able to get it down. There was no way on Earth I was going to be picky. The only time I turned down food was when I physically couldn't get it down without throwing it up. So when I heard a man in line for a local restaurant complain that he didn't like anything on the menu when it was also his first time there and hadn't yet tried anything, I found myself actually beginning to become angry. But then I reminded myself that, even if it wasn't with food, I had done plenty of similar things throughout my life.

That got me thinking, though, about just what makes us care about certain things too much. Then I went back to my foundation and my purpose. When I examined most things, I found that in reality they have little to no meaning, or at least much less than what I had thought they do. I thought about all of the different things that I used to place my identity in and I realized just how fragile they really were. I used to play football, and for a while I was known for that. Then I left. I was always one the tallest kids in my class, and I was known for that until I got to high school with much older guys, and suddenly I wasn't known for my height anymore. Then I did theater and was known for that, but even theater has come to an end. I have been known for my voice, for my beard, for my cancer battle, for being an American, and a Southern one at that, and more. However, my voice can be lost, my hair has been lost, and my cancer battle has only made up a small portion of my life, while even nations don't last forever.

At the beginning of this book, I listed a bunch of introductions, all of the labels of my identity. But the reality is that every single one of them doesn't mean anything when looked at through the lens of the grand scheme of life. When I looked through the big-picture lens, I found that a great many things I had cared deeply about, things that had been so important to me, and things that had given me a sense of purpose and meaning were ultimately trivial and finite in their impact. The more I look around, the more I see this, and it would be perhaps my biggest message to the public. What you think matters ultimately probably doesn't. That may seem like a harsh reality, but it is probably true. It was true when I took a look around. I examined my life, and the only thing that I could find meaning in was what is eternal. If there is no such thing as God, then my actions in this life will have all been in vain.

You see, I looked at my life and asked myself, if I had died, or if I do soon, what would my purpose here have been? My purpose cannot be for financial gain, because I will never be the richest person, and even if I were, what would be the point? Most people would say that you attain money to have a comfortable life, but I do not know of anyone who has not experienced brokenness. If money cannot solve brokenness, perhaps my goal would to be the smartest, except that I am not, or to get that certain job I have always envisioned, or to marry the specific person I want to. But will any of these have any significance beyond my life? Am I even guaranteed these things?

I had a friend come to me once frustrated with life, but his purpose was resting in the hope of landing a particular job. It was this hope that was driving him through the difficult times, and I asked him, "If your life were to end a week from now, or even if you were to live a long life but not attain that job, what will your life have been worth? Even if you do get this job, you will not have it forever; it will only be yours for a chunk of time in your life, so can it be what you are investing your life's purpose in?" This took my friend aback, and it may seem cruel to have poked a hole in what was driving him forward, but I wanted him to notice how fragile that hope really was in the hopes that it would prompt him to look for a deeper, more real, more true meaning.

I am guilty of placing too much purpose in relationships. Now, I must be careful in what I say, because I do believe there is tremendous worth in relationships, but if someone stakes their life's purpose on another human being, what do you have when they leave your life, as inevitably people will? As important as relationships are, and they are extremely important, one person cannot be your purpose for living. Romeo and Juliet should have taught us enough about the consequences of holding someone in that high of regard.

You might be wondering what I think does matter. It is here that every person across history has tried to come up with an answer. As a Christian, I am of course of the persuasion that a person called Jesus walked this Earth and gave the right answers. I am convinced that there is a God and that he determines meaning, and that our ultimate purpose is to be in a relationship with him. However, if I say atheism is correct, then everything I do is in vain because it has no real meaning other than the pretend meaning we assign to it. It doesn't matter how much racism is combatted or how much I am selfless to another human or how much love I give or how much support I give or my happiness or how much suffering I endure, because, regardless of human advancement or the lack thereof, the universe will cease to exist in the future and that will be that. In that case, it would be my goal to make my life as good as possible, and if my life weren't good then there would be no reason to exist in discomfort. But because I believe in God, I endure my suffering because, while it may not be fun, I know there is meaning and purpose in it greater than myself.

I do not believe that God is made happy by suffering and death,[3] but that he is actually working to end it. While he is working,[4] I will endure the race. I find meaning in relationships because the God I serve finds people meaningful. You see, either there is a God and things have meaning because he gives them meaning, or there is no real meaning at all. And if there is truly such a thing as eternity, why in the world would I waste my time worrying about things such as clothing or cars or money or being superior to others? Very little of what I often end up worrying about will matter in the long run. I do not place my identity in being a former football player or cancer survivor or American because none of these things will matter in eternity. What will matter, and what does make an eternal difference, is my identity as a servant of God, and the conversations and relationships that I foster, not for my benefit but for the benefit of all people to know God personally as I believe they can.

I also think that if people were to focus their minds and care on what is eternal, there would be a lot less fear and anxiety. When we complain about the inconveniences in everyday life, or our day becomes ruined because something doesn't go right, we often do this because we are placing too much weight on things that don't deserve it. I have realized that everything

---

3. See Ezekiel 33:11.
4. See Revelation 21:3–4.

is eventually lost, whether it be wealth, intelligence, even life itself. But if I stop placing my purpose and meaning in the finite and impermanent and refocus on the everlasting and the permanent, my whole outlook on life begins to slowly change.

I think if we are brutally honest with ourselves, we will each see that we have areas where we care too much about something or place our identity and purpose in something that ultimately won't matter. I certainly have had to reevaluate which things hold meaning in my life, but now that I have, I am much more thankful, much more joyful, and much more satisfied. It is not an easy thing to do, as I often find myself slipping back into nearly having my day wrecked because something does not go my way, but then I remind myself that while my frustration or hurt is often valid, it should not be my master because what I am upset about doesn't have eternal consequence. That could even be stress from running late, but sometimes I just need to take a moment to realize that it doesn't matter as much as I feel it does.

The idea of assigning worth is a concept that we all wrestle with over the course of our lives and is something that I believe my generation is having to fight in the realm of social media as well, where who we are is put on display and others determine our value and meaning. One of my friends sums up this idea in an honest post she made just as I was writing this chapter:

> I never post things like this because I know they don't get many likes. Why is this my first thought? I can tell you, bc I'm a self-centered, sinful person. We all are. It's the ugly truth.
>
> I don't post certain things because I think people won't like them or comment on the post. I make sure my shoes always match my outfit otherwise I feel self-conscious. I feel uncomfortable when I wear an outfit that I think "cool girls" wouldn't wear. I feel inferior to others because I'm not in a certain sorority. My first thought when trying out for things is "will this make me more cool?" and the reality is that none of this matters. *None of it.*
>
> It doesn't matter what position I have, what clothes I wear, what pictures I post or don't post, or whether my shoes coordinate with my outfit. The only thing that really matters is that God loves me and you and everyone even if you don't believe in Him.
>
> He loves with a love that has no boundaries and no limits. He has a grace that covers every aspect of our lives and our minds can't even comprehend this bc no person on this earth can do anything close to what God does for us.
>
> I was listening to my friend's worship playlist this morning and started tearing up because God has blessed me with so

much. I have the most amazing, loving, and caring friends who encourage and love me and admonish me when I get lost. I have a beautiful family that adopted me and gave me this amazing life.

I have so much and the best thing is that until I leave this earth, He will still bless me.[5]

I think Olivia sums up beautifully in a short post that which I am taking a chapter to explain. Ultimately, we care about a lot of things that pale in comparison to the God that is more real and more true than the finite things of this life. Now, I will say sometimes I need to do the opposite. Sometimes I like to brush off a test as though it doesn't matter. Tests are a great example of something people either place too little or too much care into. For some, it doesn't matter at all, and for some, their weeks or months are ruined by one bad exam. Oftentimes students swing the pendulum between these two extremes, but the reality is that, as with most things, the best response is found in the middle. The test does matter, as, again, if there is eternal significance to our actions and our hearts, then that trickles down into how we conduct ourselves. However, while it matters, a test does not determine who you are and it is not worth your heart, mind, and soul. Oftentimes we care too little or too much in just about every area of our lives. That is why I think it is so imperative that we always evaluate our lives for what truly has meaning, what our purpose really is, and adjust ourselves accordingly.

Many people realize that the things they once put purpose into have no meaning, and swing the pendulum far to the other side and resort to hedonism or some form of it. Often the mantra goes, "If it doesn't make you happy, it wasn't meant to be; move on from it." But I am living proof that life doesn't operate that way. More often than not, all of us will have to endure something we do not find happiness in to make ourselves better. Whether it is eating broccoli instead of chocolate cake or getting chemotherapy to stop cancer instead of continuing freshman year, many things that are better for us do not bring us happiness, but we must endure. I think we all need chemotherapy in some sense. To endure hardships, letting the bad parts of ourselves die in order to truly live.

Happiness here on Earth is not permanent, and therefore it is not my purpose on Earth. Don't get me wrong; I am not advocating that life is meaningless. Rather, quite the contrary: I believe that life has meaning and that what has meaning should be invested heavily into. I am merely saying that what truly has meaning, and where your purpose and identity lies, may

5. Olivia Schaffner, Instagram post, May 11, 2021, https://www.instagram.com/p/COwPFq8tOSA/?utm_medium=copy_link.

be different than what you initially put it into. I know that was at least the case for me.

We are all pursuing something. We can say our purpose is to be kind and make the world a better place, but then again I would ask, why is that important to do? Whatever it may be, there is a reason that we all get up in the morning and do what we do. I no longer see the point in pursuing things that do not last if there are things I can pursue that will last forever. It just so happens I believe that there are things that are bigger than our narrow view of our slice of life. I believe that there is such a thing as the gift of eternity and a God behind all of this, and especially coming away from cancer, recognizing how fragile my life is, and knowing one day I will pass away from here, how can I not put my time, energy, and investment into what truly matters?

"Our greatest fear should not be of failure but of succeeding at things in life that don't really matter."[6]

6. Chan and Yankoski, *Crazy love*, 90.

Peace

I wanted to take a moment to talk about peace. Throughout my time in the hospital and in the months afterward, there naturally was a lot of concern and a lot of stress. I would be shocked and slightly worried if there were not any, since I have been in a life-threatening situation, after all. But looking back, one thing I notice is the peace that not only myself but my family had throughout these months. Part of it, I think, was just that we were all in crisis mode, but I also remember each of us having individual conversations within the first two weeks, when we didn't know if my chemotherapy was working, where each of us had an unnatural peace that I would be alright. And I was.

This may or may not be encouraging to you, dear reader, but it was a significant part of my journey. Much of my time in the hospital was not spent in stress or turmoil, or worry about the future. Rather, I had peace, and that allowed us to laugh and have high spirits in a time that is generally the complete opposite. I can truly say that what should have been the darkest of times has been an emotional bright spot in my life. Would I want to repeat a hospital stay? No, but while I was there I was shown love by others, and as I took a good look at my life and realized that despite the pain there was beauty and hope, I could not help but come away from the experience joyful and content.

I said in my first post since my diagnosis that the year so far has been crazy but good. To anyone else but me, I'm sure that sounds insane and they will dismiss it as unrealistic optimism, but I say it has been true. I cannot walk away from the peace that has been given to me, the appreciation for the pure ability to wake up each and every day, and the people who are around me who have loved and sacrificed for me. That does not mean I have not had my fair share of stressful days or moments, but in spite of all the stress we could, and probably should, have had, we have been able to find peace and I do not take that for granted.

The Void

There are few things more painful to me than the feeling of loneliness. Throughout my life, I have always battled the feeling of depression I get when I feel lonely. Growing up, I was never the best at making friends, and while I was in elementary school I was generally on the bottom rung of the social totem pole. I have a mild form of Asperger's, which I have worked to overcome. Asperger's has made it difficult at times to understand social cues, but I do not see it as an excuse. Rather, I have worked to put myself in situations that force me to be social and to work to understand social cues better. Doing theater was great for me in this aspect, as I was forced to tap into my own emotions, understand emotional situations, and learn how to respond accordingly in a fantasy situation, which helped me develop in those areas in the real world. I was also surrounded by people who were, as I like to call them, social athletes. They were quick to come up with jokes or witty responses and even though it was difficult for my brain to compute at first, over time I learned how to adapt.

However, despite my willingness to work beyond Asperger's, I still struggled socially growing up. I never had a good friend group for very long until I made it to high school. I had small groups of good friends in theater or football, but it always ended up that once the show was over or the season had ended, so did the friendships. I longed for friends who were not just seasonal but would be there for me in all aspects of my life. I finally got a taste of that desire during my junior year of high school, when a solid friend group formed. For the first time in my life, I truly had people to talk to, to hang out with on the weekends, and to experience fun adventures with. Being able to finally experience a good friend group that lasted more than a few months was amazing, but it was even harder on me when it fell apart after my breakup. Once again, I was left feeling lonely on most days, but this time I had a taste of what it was like to not feel that way, which made it worse.

Now, I would like to take a moment to note that I have never been truly alone. I have always had friends and family who have been there for me, but that hasn't always chased away the voice that looms inside of me that I am unwanted. Unfortunately, walking this journey through cancer has not cured anything in this department. While I have seen some of the best of humanity as people have gone out of their way to be there for me, I have also found that many people who told me they would be there for me have not. It has not just been one person, either.

You see, the difficult thing about cancer that often goes unnoticed is the loneliness that is felt by not only the patient but oftentimes the surrounding family as well. Cancer creates several new social dynamics that are difficult to navigate, no matter which angle you approach them from. Some cancer patients, in an effort to not make themselves a burden to others as well as with a new sense of mortality and not wanting to hurt anyone by getting close, will draw back from others. It is also difficult for those around the cancer patient to know quite what to do or say. There is one side that wants to help and be there, but also the other side that doesn't know if the person even wants to talk about it. The reality is that it is different for every person, so it is hard even for me to answer as to what anyone should do. I have found that it helps me to talk about it, but even that desire has created some issues. The problem is that cancer is a really heavy subject, and the people around you may struggle with hearing all the updates and issues you are experiencing. When that happens, there may be guilt that arises in both the person with cancer and the person supporting them.

It is hard as a cancer patient not to feel guilty and a burden to others, and I have found that as time has gone on I have talked to people about my feelings less and less because I have seen people grow distant from me. After all, they have had a hard time dealing with it. But I also know that has created the feeling of guilt in them for not being there for me when I have needed it, and if I am honest, I do need the support. A cycle of difficult emotions is created, and even with good communication to one another the social situation can be a difficult one to navigate.

With cancer, there also are issues of attention withdrawal. You go from not talking to many people to having almost everyone you have ever known in your life reaching out to you and offering support while you are in the hospital, but in my experience it was not the hospital that was the most emotionally difficult. It was coming home. Once I came home, most of the support I had received in the hospital faded away, but I was still in the midst of my cancer battle, and still am. Again, this I believe is because there is a difficult social dynamic when it comes to how much privacy people think they should give me; people don't know how much I want to talk about my experiences or how much they should distract me.

It is also difficult for me to listen to people's gripes about common things, and that makes it difficult as well. When your life is dominated by cancer, it is difficult to hear people complain about shoes or hairdos. Don't get me wrong; if you are having a serious problem, I want to listen to that very badly. If there is some relationship, life, or faith crisis, I would love to hear about it and talk about it. Often people think that bringing up serious topics burdens me, but in fact it makes me feel better to help someone else with their problem. It both makes use of what I am going through and takes away from me focusing on my issues. What is difficult to listen to is people complaining about simple life problems, but I wish people would tell me more about serious problems. Typically I get the usual, "You have too much on your plate to worry about my problems," but, believe me, I would much rather listen to your problems than ruminate over my own.

When you have cancer, life slows down incredibly for you. I went from having three jobs and being a full-time student to having only one job for which I worked from home on Mondays and Tuesdays. It isn't like I could physically work more at the moment, so life ends up being slower than the pace of normal life. This can make it difficult when it comes to social life because now you have all of this free time but others do not. This free time can leave me asking others when they would like to hang out, but often they are unavailable.

While cancer has certainly added new twists in my social dynamics, I must acknowledge that, at its foundation, I cannot blame it for my social struggles. My feelings of isolation and loneliness are ultimately a heart issue. It always seems that every time I begin to complain and ask God to take away my loneliness, I will get an offer to hang out with random friends, or someone will send over a care package. I am reminded that there are people who do truly care about me and that when I have these feelings of loneliness and being unwanted, I need to not let those thoughts sit in my brain, because they are untrue. I am not saying this is easy for me in any aspect. I have had more emotional pain from loneliness than from anything else in my life, and that includes cancer. I have battled with it throughout my life, and this year has been no different. But it is important to remember that what we feel is not always true, and even though my feeling of loneliness should be felt and not suppressed, it has no business dominating my life.

I would be lying if I said that even recently it has been easy to battle against the feelings of loneliness. My church's college ministry just took a big trip down to Florida during the week when I was feeling the worst side effects of my chemotherapy. It was difficult to watch everyone talk about how they were having their favorite times of the year while I was at home unable to even stand up for long on some days. Even now that everyone has returned, it has been hard to be able to hang out with many people because, as is common in college, people want to play spikeball or volleyball or something of the sort, and I am just physically unable to. I certainly have thoughts that while some people are forming lifelong friends and having the best times of their lives I am falling behind, but it is often at these times that someone who has not reached out in a long time will check in on me or ask to come to spend time with me. It is these times that people spend with me, whether it is over coffee, lunch, or coming over to my apartment, that truly mean more to me than they realize. In this particular case, I was, in a sense, slapped in the face about my own self-pity. In the midst of me feeling sorry for myself for not being able to go to Florida, I received a note from someone who was able to go because I was not, and while I still wished that I could have gone on the trip, I realized even in this simple situation how bad things can be turned around for benefit. If God can use my suffering in this small way, surely he can use it to draw people closer to him.

I also find it difficult to talk about the future on my end. In college you are constantly talking about what your plans are for the future, and before I would have responded with an in-depth plan. However, this past semester has not only caused those plans to become uncertain, but I am honestly just trying to make it to the five-year cure mark. I have a rough outline for my future, but if this year has taught me anything, it is that the future is not guaranteed like I once imagined it was, but that is hard to say over a lunch conversation.

I have had a person recently who is older but single tell me that they could be content to be single for the rest of their life if God would take away the desire for a relationship. They have asked me if they think God will ever answer their prayer to take away the desire, and, if I am honest, I have sometimes had the same prayer. I have certainly wished that God would take away the desire to be in a relationship if that is not in my future, or take away my desire to have a group of close friends if that is not going to be the case. I have certainly prayed many, many times for God to take my loneliness away. While I do not know if the prayer will be answered, I am inclined to think not. You see, I believe that God uses that intense desire placed in us to not only be known but be known intimately, to have someone to love and to be loved, and to have someone know us to our core—that is precisely the need, or perhaps the void, that we humans ought to turn to God for. Sometimes God allows us to be brought to the place where we have nothing and no one else to turn to so that we have no option but to turn to him. Often we will turn to other things or people to try to fill that void, but it doesn't work. Ultimately, we are designed to be known and in relationship with our Creator, who knows us more intimately than anyone else and loves us so much he was willing to die for us.

We hear these words so often, but when we truly think about what it means to have a Creator, no one could know us better. He is the one who satisfies that desire that we often wish was taken away. Our pain is the unignorable call that points to the personal relationship we were all designed to be a part of. We may not always feel that, and we may always wrestle with that desire until the day we meet him face to face, but we can rest assured that the desire has a purpose and that one day it will be fulfilled. Ultimately, human relationships are meant to show us a small glimpse of God's desired relationship with us, so I don't think he would take that desire away; rather, he wants us to call upon him to fulfill that longing for relational satisfaction.

> And out of that hopeless attempt has come nearly all that we call human history—money, poverty, ambition, war, prostitution, classes, empires, slavery— the long terrible story of man trying to find something other than God which will make him happy.[7]

7. Lewis, *Mere Christianity*, 49.

Staring at a Closed Door

Once I returned from the hospital, life was obviously not the same anymore. I physically still needed to rest as my body recovered from the chemotherapy. I was and still am to this day heavily immunocompromised, meaning I have virtually no immune system. This meant that hanging out in large groups, eating raw foods such as sushi or steak, and even getting some sort of COVID vaccine was off the table for me until I fully recovered. This also meant that many of the jobs I had previously been working at would no longer be an option for me. Before my diagnosis, I worked three jobs and was a full-time student. However, I took the semester off from college because I was already ahead and was going to be very busy with follow-up chemo treatments. I could not return to my extended day work, and my work with radio had to dwindle for quite some time. This left only my newspaper job, which I could do from home, which I work Mondays and Tuesdays. That left the rest of my week free.

The problem was that mentally I felt like I was able to do things, but once I began to stand up and walk around I quickly became tired. That is the cycle I have been in to this day. One week I am in Birmingham getting chemo, the next week I am often tired and getting blood transfusions, the next week I am still tired, and then finally by the end of the third week I am nearly recovered before it is time to go back to Birmingham. This schedule has left me unable to do many activities that most college students my age are doing, but I still have had the free time. In fact, I have had much more free time than I was used to since COVID. If you recall how I handled my free time during COVID, you will remember how much of a struggle that period of time was for me, and after I got back from the hospital I have faced that struggle once again.

Not only is having free time difficult for me, but all the new layers that I mentioned above forced me to accept that I would have to be content in resting and I would have to give up my fast-paced lifestyle. It was also a struggle for me because I felt that I had moved so much spiritually while I was in the hospital. I was staring down death, after all, and I had newfound energy for life, a love for people, and I wanted to share my hope with others. However, as is common when God is working, I was not able to do what I wanted to do in the way I imagined I should be able to do it.

I spent weeks asking God why I had the passion to share and minister, with certainly plenty of time to, but there were no doors opening. Despite my frustrations, I remained vigilant to not make the same mistake that I had made prior to my diagnosis. You see, I often spent so much time focusing on my significant-other relationship, and asking God to open up doors there, that I missed the work he was doing in other areas of my life. Slowly but surely, opportunities arose in day-to-day conversations, over lunch or other outings, to talk about faith, life, and meaning. I saw quickly how the Lord answered my prayer, just not in the way I was expecting.

In the meantime, I once again had to wrestle with doing nothing. Again, this may not be a problem for you, dear reader, but it certainly was a problem for me. I was grappling with my desire to be in a different situation and learning how to rest. I had to learn how to take the free time that was given to me and devote it to God. I reminded myself that throughout the Bible there are times of rest and meditation before work is done. So I began to change my perspective on free time. I stopped trying to look to the ideal future that I wished was my present and rather began to mold my actions in the present to prepare myself for whatever future lies ahead for me. In my case, that meant using my free time to honor God in whatever way I could. From reading the Bible, to playing worship music, to spending hours diving into apologetics material and learning from some of the great teachers of our time, I began equipping myself with knowledge, and more importantly drawing closer to God in the same way you draw closer to anyone you are in a relationship with: by devoting your life to them. Even though I have sometimes reverted to wanting my busy schedule back, I have continuously become more comfortable with having free time and have learned how to utilize it to pursue what truly matters and not waste the time that is given to me.

Appreciation

I will never forget the feeling of finally leaving the hospital. It was a joyous occasion not only because it was something I had not been guaranteed, but because I had not been outside in a month. As I rode home, I kept telling my mom, "This is great!" throughout the simple car ride. And it was great. It was a nice clear day, I could move around all I wanted, and I could breathe in the fresh air. When I got home, I was able to go to the bathroom without dragging in a machine, and I could roll over in my own bed again. COVID had certainly made me appreciate the simple things in life, but my hospital stay taught me appreciation tenfold. I began to realize just how much I really had been taking for granted.

You never really know how important something is to you until you lose it. For example, growing up as a kid in a Christian home, I always was taught to thank God for the food before eating it. That always came in the form of a quick, "Dear Lord, thank you for this food in Jesus' name. Amen." If you wanted to go longer, you could always thank him for other things, but then everyone else who was hungry might start throwing side glances at you. But since my hospital stay, I legitimately thank him for the food I eat, no longer out of habit or because it is the rule a good Christian should follow, but because I now know what it is like to be physically unable to eat, and so I am truly thankful for the opportunity to eat. Likewise, I thank him every time I go to sleep for letting me have a full night's rest, for being able to have such a nice bed, even for being able to roll over in bed, because those were all scarcities in the hospital. I have my fair share of days that are hard, but when do, I always take a step back and realize that I have eaten that day, I got up and walked out of my room, I was able to go outside, and I was able to shower without having to ask a nurse for permission or wrapping my arm up in a sleeve. When I remember all of the great gifts that I often even now take for granted, it makes the problems of the day shrink.

I think that my journey through cancer, if nothing else, has made me a more appreciative person. It is also why I don't think it is bad for people to experience, at least for a short time, what growing up without excess money is like. When you do, you begin to appreciate what you do have instead of feeling entitled to what you possess. When we think of "entitled," we often cringe and become defensive when it is used to describe us because it has such a derogatory connotation. When we picture someone who is entitled, we often picture a rich person who whines and complains when they can't have something that we have often gone without. For example, you might picture a person who complains that their parents didn't get them the new car they wanted. But might I suggest that we, especially referring to Americans, are often more entitled than we think we are.

I would not have considered myself entitled at all, but at the same time I would have been upset if I had not gotten a car when I was sixteen. If I were unable to eat, I would have considered it a great travesty, rather than viewing the ability to eat as a gift each time. If I was not entitled, then I was at least ungrateful about many of the simple gifts of life. I have seen ungratefulness from even some of the strongest people I know when they were devastated upon losing some of their best possessions. Often I think that this ungratefulness springs from two things: valuing possessions more than what they are worth and expecting the comforts of your way of life rather than seeing them as a gift. When these two things become part of our mindset, we often lose thankfulness and become attached to what we have.

I would even take this idea to the level of our very own life. When we come to expect that we will live and that we will be healthy, we will be even more devastated when the reality of death and sickness meet us. Rather, a posture of thankfulness for even the most simple of comforts is something that was not natural for me, but it has become a part of my daily routine and my life has been better because of it. Besides, if you believe there is a God behind all of this, then you ought to be thankful because everything truly is a gift. That is the way I see it. Even though I was not always as thankful as I should have been, and probably still am not even now, I now see how much of my life I took for granted and that makes me more and more thankful each day. I have the ability to wake up and live another day of life when I am certainly not guaranteed tomorrow.

Parent's Perspective: Mom

My parents have had to endure many trials as well. In the hospital, they had the same lack of sleep as I did, but they were also the ones who got me food and water when I could not, they did not have as nice of a place to sleep as I did, nor did they have the emotional support that I did, and they had to drive many hours on the road while I was in the hospital as they tried to juggle work, my other siblings, and being there for me. In the months following my hospital stay, my mother has had to endure many more road trips and many five o'clock mornings followed by late nights, and while I am catered to while getting chemo or blood, she has always had to sit there just as long as me, in much less comfortable chairs and with fewer amenities. She and the nurses bring me blankets if I am cold, I am always given a nice heated chair to sit in, and I am always offered drinks, whereas she is not offered much more than drinks and the occasional snack. But through love and care, my parents have endured a hardship greater than most parents must endure. They struggle with many of the same new social issues that I spoke about in my loneliness chapter, but through it all they have found the time to laugh with me, a way to enjoy our trips, a way to bring me light in the darkness.

Ultimately, I think that has been one of the most beautiful things about this experience. Not even cancer has kept my family from laughing, from feeling some peace, from experiencing joy and happiness. Sure, it has not been easy, as indicated by my list above, but don't think for a second that I am complaining. When you have had to surrender everything, and when life situations have not been easy, but you can still smile and have joy, it is then that I think you can see what real beauty in life is.

I asked each of my parents to contribute a single chapter to this book in the hopes that, as my story may aid someone struggling, their stories may aid the often-forgotten caretakers and guardians of those who are enduring suffering. Without further ado, I would like you to be introduced to my mother, Jennifer. This is her story:

❖ ❖ ❖

January 16, 2021—the day our world flipped upside down. That morning, Matt and I were sitting in the doctor's office laughing, reading funny articles, and making jokes when the doctor walked in with a look on his face that let you know immediately that something was wrong. As he read off Matt's lab results, I knew this was bad. I had worked in health care too long not to know what those combinations of numbers meant. I sat there trying to not have a reaction for Matt's sake, but I could not stop the tears from falling down my face. The doctor told Matt and me that the lab results were bad enough that Matt would need to be sent directly to a hospital in Birmingham—either Children's of Alabama or UAB, whichever one could get him in first. We sat there not really speaking. Just texting family and friends with an update. I was trying to think of something comforting to say to Matt. Worried that if I spoke it would betray the fear I was feeling. Then I got a phone call from someone I had been friends with pretty much my whole life. She's one of those friends who has always been there for me when my life was in crisis, and here she was again. She's also a nurse. Just the sound of her voice made me cry because I realized I had someone to support me at that moment when my world was crashing. I don't even remember what she said, other than "I'm on my way." And she was. She came to the doctor's office and sat with us until the doctor was able to arrange Matt's admission to UAB.

What I remember after that was how crazy it was to go home and take a shower and pack. Everything seemed so unreal, but at the same time I couldn't help breaking down and crying. Fortunately, no one else was home because my "crying" was more of a wailing. Somehow, I managed to get packed and went to pick up Matt. Once again, I was trying to be strong for Matt. I was trying to be positive but thinking the whole time, "This can't be real!"

Thankfully, on the two-hour ride to the hospital we got a phone call from Matt's former pediatrician. Someone had told him what was going on and he talked to me for a while about Matt's lab results. He asked me what I thought was going on and I told him, "leukemia." He said I was probably right and then reassured us that, yes, this was scary, this was not great news, but the likelihood of Matt coming through treatment with a positive result was high just based on his age. This phone call was such a comfort but it also helped me mentally prepare for what came ahead. When the doctor did come in later that night and confirmed that Matthew indeed had leukemia, I wasn't surprised and I was able to speak clearly with the doctor about what the next steps for Matt would be. What was so crazy about that day for me was going from laughing and joking at ten a.m. to seeing my son surrounded by nurses at five p.m. to officially receiving a cancer diagnosis at eleven p.m. In less than twelve hours our lives changed completely.

Most days that Matt was in the hospital, I was doing okay. We had so much support, with people calling and texting often, and the days stayed busy with all the nurses in and out. But there were also those difficult, unbearable days. One of the most difficult days was when Matt found out he had AML (acute myeloid leukemia), not ALL. We were so hopeful that he would have the leukemia that has a higher success rate of being treated that when we found it was AML it felt like being kicked in the chest. Google which type of leukemia is most fatal and there AML will be staring you in the face. And then, to make things worse, right after receiving this devastating news the doctors came in to do Matt's first bone marrow biopsy. I tried to stay in the room while they did the procedure, but as they started prepping Matt for the biopsy I knew I was about to lose it. I quickly left the room and ran down the hall to the public restroom room and I couldn't hold it in any longer. I know that anyone walking down the hallway heard me crying because, again, this was not crying, it was wailing from the pain I was feeling and the pain that my son was experiencing and the pain he would experience.

Somewhere during my parenting journey, I picked up this deep-down belief that if I loved my kids deeply enough that would be enough to give them a good life. As mothers, we become accustomed to being able to kiss our kids boo-boos away, to wipe away their tears, to give them a hug and make their hurt go away. But this was something I couldn't fix. I couldn't make this better. I couldn't kiss this pain away. And what made this worse was that not only was Matt hurting, but my other two children were hurting too from the worry and stress over their brother. For the first couple of months, I couldn't even say the word "cancer" when it was related to Matt. I could say "Matt has leukemia" but I could not say "Matt has cancer." It was too painful and too scary.

Watching Matt go through this journey is probably the hardest thing I have been through. It wasn't the fact that he had cancer. I never had the thought "Why Matt?" because, quite honestly, why anyone? No one deserves to have cancer—to undergo the stress, the pain, and the fear that comes along with a cancer diagnosis. But watching my child, who had always been so healthy and strong; my child, whom I had raised and loved so dearly, suffer like this was a new type of pain that was almost unbearable. This was a pain and hurt that I had never felt before and it overwhelmed me so much at times that I could hardly function.

I would try to work and would just stare at my computer, just wanting to go to sleep. When Matt was at the hospital in Birmingham undergoing chemo, I was the one who was having to take a nap every day, not my son, who was receiving the chemo. When I was home, I felt so guilty because there were times that I should have been spending time with my other two kids but instead I would just sleep. I distanced myself from my friends, not because they didn't want to spend time with me or they weren't sympathetic to what we were experiencing, but because there was not really anything else going on in my life. So I felt like when I was interacting with others I would have to fake that everything was okay, because who wants to be a downer all the time? I also just really couldn't open up to anyone about how difficult everything was.

We are usually a family that attempts to find humor in the everyday craziness of life. We pick on each other a lot and make fun of situations that would normally stress most people out, and we attempted to do the same thing in this situation. But this just wasn't funny. Yes, we would make jokes about Matt losing his hair or Matt would make a joke about how long it would take for him to walk somewhere, but, deep down inside, what Matt was having to go through just wasn't anything I could find humor in. Matt is six feet two, strong, and has pretty much always been healthy. And now he was only able to take a few steps without getting short of breath. I watched my son experience being scared of what this diagnosis was going to mean for him, not knowing if he would live through cancer, finding out that the chemo would make him sterile; watched my nineteen-year-old son deal with losing every expectation that he had for his future, and watched as my child who had always been goal-oriented withdrew from school. As he received more courses of chemo, I watched my strong, independent son lose his hair and not be able to walk more than a few steps at a time. He became so fatigued at times that he had a difficult time just doing everyday tasks. On top of that, his brother and sister were scared and hurting too. I felt completely helpless and lost.

Matt is a great big brother. Don't get me wrong; he loves picking on his siblings and he knows exactly how to get them agitated. But he is also protective of and kind to them. When he moved out of the house to his college apartment, he wrote each one of us a letter telling us how much we meant to him. Every day he was in the hospital, or when he would have to get lab work or transfusions, he would ask the nurses how their days were, ask them how they were doing, and somehow his kindness to everyone while he was going through painful procedures made it harder for me to watch.

During the last round of chemo that Matt received, he almost became too sick to receive the chemo he needed. During that week, there was one night that Matt was scheduled to receive chemo and the nurses had to stick him five times to get IV access. I finally just lost it. I started crying right there in the infusion room in front of the nurses and just could not stop the tears. This must not have been the first time a thing like that had happened in there, because none of the three nurses said anything about it. They just kept on working on Matthew.

After Matt's last round of chemo at the end of April, his chemo side effects were probably at their worst. He had sores in his mouth, chemo rash on his head and face, and shortness of breath when he walked. This was probably when I hit my lowest point. I had pretty much withdrawn from everyone in my life except my mother and my kids and I was deeply depressed. One night, when I was almost to my breaking point, I was texting my sister and she must have asked about Matt. I'm not sure how our conversation started or what I said, but my sister ended up saying the one thing I think I had been waiting for someone to say to me this whole time. She told me that I had had to be strong throughout this situation for Matt and for AJ and Emma, so I should let her be the one who was strong for me. These were the exact words I needed to hear at the time, and I unloaded every hurt and burden on her that I had been carrying around for the past four months. My sister, being the person that she is, provided me words of comfort and then came up with an action plan to get me more emotional support. The thing is, I didn't really need it after that. I just needed to know that someone was there for me if I ever needed to unburden myself again.

So how has this changed me? What have I learned? I am definitely closer to my mom and to the few friends who have been by my side during this journey. I am trying to be more present in my daily life and focus on having quality time with my kids. Now, two months after Matt's official report that he was in remission, he for the most part has gone back to his normal routine and life. His hair and beard have grown back. He looks healthy again, but I am still very much changed by this experience. I have still distanced myself from people.

Before, I would get upset or angry at people that had come into my life and that I had gotten close to and then, for whatever reason, our friendship or relationship ended. But now I am really beginning to understand that whole Madea speech, where Madea explains that some people in our lives are like leaves—they come and go—while some people are like branches— just meant to be in our lives for a season, to help us through a certain period in our lives—and that's okay. Holding on to bitterness and anger is such a waste of your time. I am attempting to feel my feelings, be okay with the feelings I am experiencing (hurt, anger, sadness), but then move on.

As for my relationship with God—I don't know. A few days after Matt was diagnosed with leukemia, I had a peace that he was going to be okay. Not that this experience would be easy, not that he wasn't going to face hardships, but that everything would be okay. In my darkest moments I would try to remember that. Kind of like holding on to a promise that I felt like God had made to us. "Us" being my mom and my other son, AJ, who both said they had experienced the same thing. But, to be honest, I haven't fully trusted God during the past few months. When Matt has been having a really bad day and I have felt like he has needed prayer, I haven't been praying for him myself. I have always been contacting women who I feel like are true prayer warriors and who I feel like have a hotline to God. But I have been scared to pray. Scared to ask him to protect my son, scared that he would say no to my prayers, because that is honestly how I have felt like God has responded to the most heartfelt prayers that I have cried out to him in the past. But after Matt was told that he was in remission, I realized that in the past I would ask God for something but then never trust him 100 percent to handle that situation. I would become impatient, think God was telling me no to something I had asked for, and I would then try to make those things happen on my own. I had never trusted God enough to completely turn my life over to him. I understand why. After being hurt or rejected so many times, it's what you expect of people. And I guess that is what subconsciously I was expecting God to do.

Even now. Even after all we have been through, and all the things in my life that God has carried me through, the thought of completely handing my life over to him scares me. And why wouldn't it? Essentially, becoming a Christian is giving up control. Giving up control of your own life and will. But here is what I do know. I know that all of this happened in God's timing. Three years ago, I reluctantly left a job I really enjoyed and changed to the one I have now. Matt aged out of his health care insurance in December 2020. Knowing this would happen, I put him on my health insurance, which became effective January 1, 2021. Matt was diagnosed with leukemia fifteen days later. The place where I'm employed is one of the insurance providers for UAB hospital, which means Matt ended up in the hospital that my insurance provider happens to have great coverage for. In addition, my job usually entails me making home visits, but in March 2020 we began working remotely due to COVID. Because of this, I was able to work from the hospital while he was there. If this had happened in any other season of my life, I wouldn't have been able to stay with Matt as much while he was at the hospital or I would have had to take leave from my job, which, as a single mother, I would have never been able to do.

The other thing I know is that God has a plan for Matt being diagnosed with cancer. I don't fully understand what that plan is and I am not even really trying to figure it all out. I have no idea what the future holds. So much of this year has been focused only on getting Matt through treatment and

I haven't had a chance to think past that. But neither Matt or I are on our same life path. He has changed his major and school and I have changed my priorities and where I focus my time and energy. In the past, I have focused on doing a certain thing (be in a relationship, take this trip, do this activity) for me to find happiness. But now I am attempting to focus more on the present by finding things each day that bring me joy—the sunset, my flowers blooming, my kids laughing—and then being grateful for those things.

Back in 2020, when Matt was going through a difficult time, I was talking to him in the kitchen and I said to him, "Look, your life is really crappy right now. I mean, it is; there is no denying that. But just because this is your reality now doesn't mean this is going to be your reality in the future." Little did I know that the reality that he would face would be much more difficult, but the point remains. Just as the high points in our life don't last, neither do the low points. Matt's reality in 2020 was not the same as his reality in 2021. His reality in January 2021 was not the same as his reality in August 2021.

2021 has by far been the most difficult year our family has ever faced. Not only because of Matt's leukemia diagnosis, but added to that were so many other life stressors and hardships that kept coming at us so often that by June I felt like I couldn't withstand one more problem in my life. I feel like I have reached my breaking point more than once this year. But, even with all that, even with all the difficult days, I am still here, our lives are still good, and I still find joy every time one of my kids laughs.

After Matt's last round of chemo, the one where he became so sick that he almost couldn't complete the chemo, we were driving home and I looked at him and noticed that his head was already breaking out in the chemo rash. I said to him, "Oh honey, your head is already breaking out," and I started to get upset. Matt looked at me and said, "It's okay. No matter what I have to go through, it's okay, Mom, because I know God's going to use this for his glory." And this is what I hold on to.

—*Jennifer Johnson*

Parent's Perspective: Dad

On the day I moved out of my house and into the apartment that would become my college home, my dad drove down with his truck and his trailer and we loaded up all my possessions and drove off to what I felt was going to be an exciting new adventure. I hopped in his truck and, as we drove the short trip over to my apartment, he asked how I had slept, and I said something to the extent of "Not so well. I was excited." I asked him the same, and he replied that he too hadn't slept well, but for another reason. "Son," he said, "I had a dream that you had cancer." I didn't know how to respond to that at the time, so I just brushed it off by saying that I was happy it was just a dream. Little did I know that five months later I would be in the hospital with cancer, and while I did not have cancer at the time, neither my dad nor I have forgotten that moment. I asked my parents to both contribute a chapter retelling their experiences as their son went through cancer. I appreciate them both doing it, because I know how hard it was for both of them to go back into that headspace, even just to write these chapters. I pray that their hardship might strengthen you, at the very least letting you know that you are not alone. This is the story as told by my father, Ryan.

❖ ❖ ❖

It is said that the production of masterpieces in literature is much like giving birth. There are great pains before its completion. Yet, I wonder if the opposite is true—that death brings forth life, that there is great darkness before great light. It is said Beethoven lost his hearing prior to composing his most famous Ninth Symphony. The world needs to pay special attention to those who have gone through great loss or even close to death's door and returned to tell a message, a great masterpiece. My oldest son, Matthew, has come close to death and his message is one that is compelling to listen to in a world where the trend is gray and the road less taken is growing with briars. Matthew asked me to share my side of the story of how I have dealt with his personal tragedy.

Many readers will remember the events that happened on September 9, 2001. I remember where I was when the towers were hit by the hijacked airplanes. Time stood still for millions of Americans that day. Regardless of all differences, it was a day we were stuck in a snapshot of memory. Very rarely does time stand still as on 9/11, and I am grateful for that. Yet, January 16, 2021 was one of those days that I remember like a snapshot of time where I was when the news came. I was home at my parent's house when I got a call from Jennifer, Matthew's mom. I could tell immediately that something was wrong by the serious tone in her voice, and she told me Matthew was very sick. Before I move on, I want to give you a reference point as to Matthew's health up to that point. A couple of weeks prior to the phone call, Matthew and I had gone deer hunting, something that we like to do together. That particular day we had gone out into the woods and Matthew had success in harvesting a buck—his first buck, that is. We drug the deer almost out of the woods and we were both laughing about how out of shape we were. We got the deer about fifty yards away from a clearing in the woods and I couldn't go anymore, looking at the terrain. I went to get the tractor and was going to pull the deer out, but by the time I got back to the edge of the woods Matthew had drug the deer out by himself and was standing there looking bored. I couldn't believe what he had done! To drag the buck out of the woods uphill, through briars, rocks, and trees was a major feat. Fast forward about a week and I learned that Matthew could barely walk up a flight of stairs to his apartment without almost passing out. The contrast was certainly worth noting. This was the context leading up to the phone call that froze time for me.

Jennifer relayed to me the news she had received from his general physician, to whom I am very grateful, that Matthew's blood panel pointed to leukemia. That word was what triggered the world to stop and my breath to halt for what seemed like hours. She told me that Matthew was very sick and they were heading right away to the University of Alabama in Birmingham (UAB). Nothing in life really prepares you for a moment like that. My first reaction after hanging up the phone was as if someone had slapped me across the face. I was in shock and disbelief. All I knew after relaying the information to my parents was to get bags packed for what could have been my last time to see my son. I tried my best to get all my essentials together in record time while it seemed the world had started to spin around me. Somehow, I got everything packed and drove to Birmingham to UAB. I have driven that part of the interstate many times, but this particular time was a blur. Several thoughts that came to me while traveling were: "This can't be true"; "Jennifer is wrong"; "Not my son!" I prayed while I was driving, pleading to God that this was the wrong diagnosis, that all this was a huge mistake. Once I got to the hospital, I met Matthew and his mom. I gave Matthew a big hug. Just to touch my son and to see him face to face was exactly what I needed. And at that moment I suspected what he needed as well.

We walked from the parking lot to the emergency room, which is not but a hundred feet. Matthew couldn't walk that distance without taking several breathing breaks in between. We got checked in to the hospital and we were sent to the hematology/oncology ward. I admit I am not a doctor, but I knew enough medical terminology to know this is not where you go if you have minor aches and pains. Reality began to set in as we got onto the eighth floor and met the nurses and staff and were given room 8221. Room 8221 was where hope was dashed for me and was the first time I heard the word "leukemia" as a diagnosis from a doctor about Matthew's condition.

The nurses and staff wasted no time in running several panels of blood analysis. The room swam with individuals who poked and prodded my son in order to figure out for sure what type of leukemia Matthew was dealing with. So many things were happening so quickly that it was difficult to reset reality time and time again. I won't rehash the details that have already been written about in previous chapters. I want, however, to give several perspectives of the journey into the crisis of my son's cancer.

There is a thought in modern counseling that says there are five stages of grief. These five stages are: denial, anger, bargaining, depression, and acceptance. Though each stage has a clear definition that sets it apart from other stages, they are not neatly separate from each other. In other words, one may be in denial and yet be dealing with depression at the same time. This has been my experience. When I first began dealing with Matthew's cancer diagnosis, I was certainly in shock and disbelief. It is hard to express what I felt during those first few hours and days after learning Matthew had cancer. I suspect in some way I was living in two separate realities. The first reality is what you experience in a day-to-day existence. Then you have another reality merging together that is extremely contrary to that day-to-day existence and threatens and tears into what you cherish the most. This was how I felt at the first stage of denial.

The next stage for me was perhaps an addition to the five stages of loss, which I call overload. I went from Christmas celebrations to now an overload in crisis. The phone call on January 16 threw me into a realm that I knew very little of. Years ago, when I was a teenager, my grandmother passed away from cancer and that was my basic extent of dealing with this tragic disease. When Matthew's diagnosis became more of a reality, there was an incredible learning curve of terminology I had never heard before.

There was a significant overload of information that you had to take in and learn because it was the enemy of your own flesh and blood.

After the overload, I seemed to go into fight mode. Being a father, there is something within you that wants to fix something that is wrong, especially an enemy seeking to take the life of your son. I wanted desperately to physically stop this enemy with my own two hands, but I couldn't. I had to rely on individuals who knew much more about how to bring victory against this enemy. In an odd way, as a dad I felt relegated to the sidelines as the medical team fought this battle. That was painful for me, especially seeing Matthew stuck and prodded multiple times a day. This led me to bargaining while I watched all this unfold. I begged God to let me be the one to suffer so Matthew wouldn't have to endure this incredible pain. I have always prided myself on reading people's faces and having an accurate understanding of what they are feeling. I would look at Matthew's face and see what just a few days ago was a strong and vibrant man, now pale as he fought for his life. It seemed like he aged ten years in just a few days. When any good parent sees their child in a similar condition, you naturally, even desperately want to trade places. In my case, there was little I could do except watch and pray. My relationship with God was put to the test and I want to shed light on this aspect of my journey.

I am not a Bible scholar, but I have several years of formal training in how to study the Bible and communicate truths about God to others. It is easy to read the Bible for the purpose of sharing to others, but it is harder to study with the goal of allowing God to speak into areas in your own life where you growth and maturity. Again, I want to remind you and myself that we never know exactly how we are going to react in crisis situations, but I do believe our previous experiences and seeing how God has taken us through less difficult hardships prepares us for the unexpected.

I like to think of our spiritual life in terms of geography. Sometimes God leads us like Jesus was led into the desert. Sometimes we find ourselves in the sweet valley beside still waters. Sometimes our journey takes us to new heights where we can look back and see from God's perspective what dangers and travesties he has kept us from. I wish I could tell you that my personal time with God was filled with praise and worship songs and sweet times of prayer. The fact is, I was numb to God at first. I did pray and I knew what to pray for but they were short, to-the-point prayers. I am not sure why praying was strenuous; perhaps it was because I was angry and afraid. Many questions came through my heart: "Does God hear my voice?" "Why has the Lord allowed this evil to come upon Matthew?" "God, are you going to heal my son?" These and many more questions I asked the Lord. I find solace in asking these questions because this can be a step toward rich growth in how we communicate and relate to God. God is big enough and secure enough for us to pose hard questions. Read the Psalms if you don't believe me. The psalmist asks questions that I don't hear many modern worships songs or even sermons address. Yet, the Psalms teach us the powerful reality that God wants a relationship with us even during life-threatening situations. This reality of invitation from the Psalms provided much support during the days of not knowing what would happen to my son, to know I am not alone.

We are not alone in our trials. The enemy wants you to believe there is no one else on the planet with problems like yours. I know that because I have had thoughts and feelings that caused me to believe I was in total isolation. In reality, I was never alone. So many people that heard the news about Matthew called to give me a word of hope, encouragement, and prayers. My close friends called me almost daily to check on the status of Matthew and how I was emotionally doing. I cannot overstate the strength I received from those conversations. This is the face of God and his touch when we receive care from others.

I have wondered why the Lord never comes in a cloud of fire and steps out from it and shows himself to us in awesome majesty. Yet Elijah, the great prophet of old, in his great weakness from trying to escape his enemies encountered the Lord. God told Elijah to hide himself in a cave as he passed by. First came a powerful windstorm with the strength to split the mountain, but God was not in the windstorm. Secondly, an earthquake came that shook his little hole in the rock, but the Bible says God was not in the earthquake. Thirdly, a raging fire came through and yet God was not in the fire. Only after these three awesome displays of power did God meet Elijah in a still, small voice. The point is that sometimes we encounter God's presence in tenderness of mercy and grace and not in the grand fashion we think God should appear in. We are reached physically and emotionally by God's servants in a phone call, a text, a hug, or even when someone is present and doesn't know what to say. This is the way I was ministered to and received God's presence through friends and family reaching out. We cannot survive without some form of community embracing us and loving us through unquestionable hardships.

Lastly, I want to share with you dear reader a psalm that helped me considerably during Matthew's fight with cancer. Closely read these words in Psalm 103:1–5:

> Bless the Lord, my soul,
> And all that is within me, bless His holy name.
> Bless the Lord, my soul,
> And do not forget any of His benefits;

Who pardons all your guilt,
Who heals all your diseases;
Who redeems your life from the pit,
Who crowns you with favor and compassion;
Who satisfies your years with good things,
So that your youth is renewed like the eagle.[8]

The psalmist wants us to be included in a great truth about how God works in our lives. It is rare for any of us to be 100 percent vulnerable with each other. It is hard to give all of ourselves to another person because we don't know if letting ourselves be fully known will be received with open arms or closed fists. Yet, this is exactly what the writer of this psalm asks us to do with the Lord. He challenges us, urges us to allow every exposed and hidden part of ourselves to be exposed before himself as a sacrifice, a praise. The "praise" itself is not about us, but about the Lord's power in his goodness, which ironically is about us.

There is a simple progression of how the Lord wants to help his children. First, the Lord "forgives all your sins." He cleans the house on the inside first, with our selfish attitudes that cause us to live imperfectly toward our fellow man. Only the Lord can forgive us because when we sin against man, we ultimately sin against God. The best part is the Lord forgives us of "all your sins." Then, only when the Lord has cleansed our inside attitudes and how we misrelate to others, does he move on to the next order of business: our diseases. What strikes me every time I read about Jesus is how much attention he spent on physical healing. In this psalm we read the same. The Lord cares about our physical healing and leaves no rock unturned. The Lord "heals all your diseases," not just some. The Lord not only forgives us of *all* our sins, but he heals *all* our diseases. Lastly, the Lord brings us out of great darkness and illness and "redeems" us. The picture of redemption is paying a high price for something that appears unvaluable. We are of high value to the Lord. Every one of us, no matter how far you have ventured away from your Father's house, has immense value to God. God desires for each of us to receive from the Lord a crown of worth with "love and compassion" and abundant gifts to the extent that our near-death existence is replaced by a great and wonderful life. So great of a life that we go from the "pit" to the air like the eagles. This is how I have seen the Lord work in so many lives and how he has worked in the life of Matthew. We all need to listen to masterpieces of those who have touched death and have come to tell us the way to fly with the eagles.

—*Ryan Johnson*

---

8. Psalm 103:1–5, NASB.

BOOK THREE

Christ

Introduction

I have not written an introduction for either of the other two sections in this book, but I feel that I should for this one. I want to acknowledge that I experience some of my most trying hardships leading up to times when I am drawn close to Christ. I have had no issue in writing on COVID or cancer, but in the days leading up to writing this section I have gone through seemingly uncaused and random depression and loneliness that has hit me out of nowhere. I felt the same way in the days leading up to my baptism just a few weeks ago, and while my faith has never been stronger since getting cancer, it is always in these times when I seem to be preparing to speak about Christ that I experience some of the hardest attacks against my mental health and my beliefs.

It is in these times that I try to step back from the emotions that threaten to consume all of my thoughts, look beyond myself to the big picture, and return to my solid foundation of why I believe what I do. I will also note that of all three sections of my story, none are more important than this one. I imagine that you may or may not agree with the premise of this entire section. Perhaps you have never believed in a deity, or perhaps you do and it is not the Christian one. Perhaps you have previously believed in Christ, but life hit you or you were hurt deeply by the legalism of the church and now you don't know what to believe. Maybe you grew up in the church but started asking questions and began a journey of not taking beliefs for granted but making them your own, but you don't know if there is a God or not. Perhaps you have always grown up in church but you don't really know why you believe what you do, and if you grew up in the Middle East you would be Islamic or if you lived in India you would be Hindu. Perhaps you call yourself a Christian but in reality you bring a lot of your own interests into the equation. Or perhaps you truly do believe that there was really a person called Jesus and that he was who he said he was and he did defy all known laws of reality in rising from the dead and because of that you have fully bought into him. Wherever you land on the spectrum, I hope that you will still be able to gain something from this third section of the book. Even if you don't, I hope that the previous two sections give you strength.

The two previous sections, COVID and Cancer, shared the story of my last year, but the story I told there does not compare to the importance of this final section. You have read how my belief in Christ has permeated my life through the trials above and how it has sustained me through them. I cannot stress the importance of Christ, and I cannot simply dismiss religion. It is too important. If I am right, it changes everything. If I am wrong, then I am a fool and all I have endured, sacrificed, and hoped for is in vain. Now, this last section will not be apologetics based or trying to win you, the reader, over to Christianity. I do love apologetics, but that is not the point of this book. I am simply sharing the different areas that I have been learning in this past year. I can already see my mother rolling her eyes at the length of this preface, so, with the above things in mind, let's dive into the good stuff.

Refreshing the Gospel

I grew up in Alabama, a part of the Bible Belt of the South. Here, most people grow up going to church, or if you don't go to church, you get some vague idea about Christian beliefs or perhaps some general ideas on what Christians believe. I will qualify the previous sentence by saying that it is becoming progressively less and less true. Much of Christian thoughts and values are permeated within our culture, but do people truly understand Christianity? The older I get, the more I feel concerned about the state of the church and the presence of church culture. What I find happening very often now is that as people grow up into the upper years of high school and college they are redefining their faith or they are leaving altogether. Some older people I know want to blame this mass exodus on the "liberal" philosophies, but this is foolish to me. The real problem that I find lies within much of the church itself.

I would compare much of the church *culture* we see today to the Pharisees and Sadducees that we find in the New Testament. These religious groups were so concerned with following the written laws of God that they created further laws to ensure that the written laws wouldn't even accidentally be violated. I see this sort of legalism playing out in the lives of many young adults today. For example, when you are young, you are taught that cussing is wrong. The justification given is often along the lines of "The Bible tells us not to" or "That's not the Christian, God-honoring thing to do." Then, as the child grows older, they are exposed to more people, more shows, and more fellow students and gradually they realize that cussing not only occurs in the world, but it is actually more common to cuss than to not. You learn the different words and how to use them, and you try them out and realize that there is seemingly no harm in using them. In fact, you will probably be more socially accepted if you do. You learn that the reality of life does not match up with what you were told as a child was right and wrong, and suddenly religion looks a lot more like a way to keep kids in line than with what reality is. Besides, the whole premise of the parents' argument was that the Bible says so, but it doesn't explicitly say I can't cuss, and even if it did, why does the Bible have authority over me? Is it actually the word of God, or a man-made construct? Besides, I see plenty of other Christian kids, men, and women cussing, so really it's just the sticklers who say I can't do that, and they don't understand reality.

I use cussing as a simple example, but the reality is that you can take out cursing and put in a host of different issues. Sex outside marriage, drugs, drinking, LGBTQ rights, or even gay marriage, abortion, views on racism and critical race theory, politics, and more. With any of these issues, often the same scenario as the one I played out with cussing occurs, and when you throw in independence and the ever-widening world of ideas and beliefs that the internet and college provide, the fields are ripe for people to leave the church and pursue their own ideas, logic, and belief systems. The response of many parents is to shelter their kids by heavily restricting internet access, laying down strict ground rules in the household, and keeping their kids only in Christian circles so that they are never exposed and molded by the influences of a non-Christian society. There are very serious flaws with this method of parenting, mainly in that you cannot shelter kids forever, and I have witnessed a lot of damage done to kids who were sheltered when the real world hit, and it hit them hard.

Some people blame the shift in mentality on colleges, on the liberal professors destroying previously solid kids' faith. This is ridiculous. What is really happening is not the fault of the "evil professors," but rather I propose that what is going on is that there is no foundation on which to rely, and so when new ideas are introduced that make logical sense—certainly more sense and more thought out than the childhood "The Bible says so"—why shouldn't people be more attracted to them? If you don't know why the Bible is trustworthy and authoritative and if there are other ideas that allow you to do what you want to do, it is easy to see why one wouldn't stick to Christianity. Especially if churchgoers cannot or will not answer your difficult questions. This process has become so common that it now has a formal name: deconstruction.

Many who grow up in the church experience a time when their faith is deconstructed or broken. Some put it back together again; some never do. I think it is good for the church to talk about the difficult questions about our faith and life, and I am thrilled when they do. But one thing I believe we must do is refresh the gospel, especially here in America. Almost everybody here has heard of Christianity in some sense or has some vague idea of what we believe. Most often, people know Christianity by our stances on topics. If I tell someone that I am a Christian, what tends to pop up in a non-Christian's head is the idea that I am against drinking (or at least the fun kind), drugs, abortion, gay marriage, partying, trans rights, etc., and immediately there is a wall placed up between us. This is because much of Christianity in America has become legalism, and we are known more for our stances on issues than our gospel.

Too often what I see is that Christians become so consumed with the issues that they forget that there is a purpose behind everyone's actions. For example, a parent might become so upset that their child has done drugs and focus so intently on the act of doing drugs that they miss the real issue, and that is the brokenness and separation from God. That separation is something we all experience. We may not all do drugs, but I guarantee even the "best" of Christians have dealt with their own issues in some way or another that is considered a sin. We all turn to different things to cope with the symptoms of the separation we all feel.

I like to use my cancer as an image to show what is happening. You see, when I had cancer, I had many side effects such as shortness of breath. Now, if I concerned myself too much with treating my shortness of breath, I would never have found the source of the issue. It was no good for me to exercise every day because that wasn't solving the real issue.

What I also see happening in some cases is that parents will see a crude joke or cussing and associate the cursing or bad joke with lack of salvation and explode on their child, causing the child to retreat and close themselves off from the parents. In these cases I think it again is wise to remember that in any case a Christian ought to present the truth but do so with gentleness and respect, always loving the other person. I know that this overblown response usually comes from love for their child, mixed with shock that the person you had a perfect image of is not perfect, but it is good to further remember that neither are we and overreactions have damaged a lot of my peers growing up and pushed them away from Christianity.

Many people I know have seriously been hurt by this cold legalism that I spoke of in the previous two paragraphs, so they swing the pendulum to progressive Christianity or leave altogether. Often the mental switch is made from the cold God who sits in the sky waiting for me to break one of his rules and to send down his wrath so I have to walk on eggshells or I will go to hell, to the all-happy Jesus who is there to help me and who would never send me to hell. Please note these are both oversimplified, but the idea is that people often drop cold legalism and switch to love-only focuses.

In other cases, Christians are shaken because they know so little about the Bible that when someone who has legitimately done some research challenges them, they are unable to respond. What I want to do in this chapter is get back to the foundation of Christianity. To take away any consumerism-driven, watered-down, prosperity-centric, legalistic gospel and get back to the truth. The reality is that in Christianity there is no God without him being a loving one, and there is no God without there being wrath. You cannot have one without the other.

The first step into seeing this God correctly is in understanding how we read the Bible, namely, in understanding that it is not a self-help guide and its purpose is not to tell you the secret of how to live in a peaceful land forever once you die. In fact, I want to dispel any ideas you might have about going to heaven. Generally, when one pictures heaven, they picture a place with some fluffy clouds and maybe some harps and if you are really good in life that's where you get to go. But that is not what the Bible describes. Rather, it talks about a New Heaven and a New Earth entirely. When you read the Bible with yourself as the focus, as the main character, so to speak, you miss out on a whole lot of things and it becomes very confusing. How in the world are these old laws to the Israelites related to me? In imagining that you are Noah, you miss out on the bigger picture that shows how God both serves his wrath and makes a way of escape. Or we see ourselves as Moses but miss out on the fact that God again provided a way—through the Passover and sacrifice of a lamb—of escape from his necessary wrath, a recurring theme throughout the Bible. You imagine yourself as David but miss the fact that David was not a parallel to you overcoming your tough situation but an example of how God can move through even a simple shepherd to accomplish his will. When you change your perspective and view the Bible not with you as the main character but with God as the main character and the Bible as the story of him revealing his character, everything begins to change. You begin to see this big, beautiful story unfold as the character of God is revealed, and then you realize we play a role in that grand story.

The gospel is simply this: that God created our world and placed us in it to rule alongside him. We chose to follow our own path, to be our own gods, and we separated ourselves and the world from him. Because of this separation, the world deserves destruction; however, God, still desiring to dwell with his creation, made a way to escape destruction through the sacrifice of Jesus Christ, God in the flesh, so that anyone who chooses to follow him can dwell with him.

He was with us at first but, because he wanted a loving relationship with us, he gave us the choice to walk away from him, and that is the choice we made and still make to this day. Because of this separation, we are caught now in a world that was once good and still retains some of those qualities but that is ultimately separated from its creator and suffering as a result. We say that God is good and holy and such, but I think we often forget what that means, especially if we grew up in church. God is not good in the sense that we call one another good. When we say that, we are merely saying that the other person is doing things that are considered good a majority of the time, or that their intentions are just. But God is the embodiment of good—the definition, so to speak—and, being the embodiment of good, he can't have a lack of goodness in his presence. He is not like, for example, the God of Hinduism, where both a person and the cancer inside him are equally reflections of the Divine. No, rather, he is a God of sides, meaning that he is good and not evil, loving generosity and hating its opposite. Because He is the embodiment of good, He cannot dwell with evil, and therefore He cannot dwell with us because we chose evil. This is the problem presented to us early on in the Bible. The rest of the Bible tells the story of how God has worked, is working, and will continue to work to set his fallen creation right again.

The Old Testament shows God teaching people about him and revealing himself to the world through them, but also shows how incapable man is of restoring itself. This is where God in the person of Christ wanted to dwell with his creation so badly that he humbled himself to become human, and not any human but a homeless servant, and not only just to humble himself but to suffer and die a horrible death. He was the ultimate sacrifice. This is the good news. That God was not content to sit on his throne and watch his creation be destroyed so he offered a way out of the chaos and wrath and a way to dwell with him. Any parent worth their salt would not let a thief break into their home and harm their child but would run to them and protect them, without regard for their own safety. That is what God did for us.

We often say that God is a God of justice and mercy and gloss over that, but, on second thought, we think surely that cannot be true. God cannot be all justice and all mercy; those are not compatible. Because God is all justice, he demands that the wrongs of the world be dealt with. However, his mercy is shown through Jesus dying on the cross. I stood before the judge guilty as charged, but the judge rose, took off his robe, and took the punishment in my place.

We don't often like to talk about God's wrath, but to not would be to deny an essential part of God, and one that actually I think we do like in a sense. People are perfectly comfortable with the idea of God serving out justice to the rapist, the murderer, to the Hitlers of the world, but as soon as the lens of wrath closes in on us, our family, and our friends, the idea of wrath becomes much more uncomfortable. We tend to justify and trivialize our wrongs and bring up why what we did in our situation was okay and why we don't deserve the full wrath. But it cannot be forgotten that, as we established, God is a good God. This should bring us both comfort and fear. Comfort in that those who have wronged me will be dealt with. Fear because I realize that I am guilty of doing wrong against my God and my fellow man and am deserving of wrath just as much as the next.

Because God is a good God, he must deal out justice. Every wrong must be accounted for. Before him, the perfect being, I will stand guilty. I deserve hell. But because he is also a merciful God, my guilt was taken on by Christ so that I may be with him, and all I have to do is pursue him. Believe in him. Therefore, the punishment has been paid, justice has been served, and God gets to dwell with his people.

However, for those who have not trusted in Christ, their guilt still rests upon them. The guilt only leaves if you accept the gift, but for those who do not accept the free gift of God, as they are free to deny, the wrath of God will still need to be satisfied. Again, this isn't a problem in many scenarios where the culprit is distant. If someone gets away with murder, we are pleased to think that God will serve justice. But when we are held under the microscope, we don't like the idea of justice so much. But to have justice, there must be punishment.

On the other hand, some people want to talk about wrath too much, and some even use the threat of hell to get people to convert to Christianity. I call this path of becoming a Christian getting your fire insurance, and I find it one of the most unbiblical practices that completely and harmfully misses the entire point of the Bible. The God we find when we read through the Bible, not with our own agendas or presuppositions, but with open eyes, is a God that is unlike any other. He is not distant in the clouds waiting for you to mess up. No, instead he wants you. He desperately wants to dwell with you, but he will never force you to be with him. And the price of not being with him is separating yourself from the pure essence of love, joy, peace, happiness, and all else that is good in the world. God's goal this entire time is to be in a relationship with us, to dwell among us. That is why at the end of times it's not just about going to heaven. No, what is described is much more beautiful than that. What is described is God remaking creation anew. The language used to describe this new creation has all sorts of callbacks to Eden. It is the picture of God coming down to live with us for eternity. That is the whole point of the Bible. God actively restoring a loving relationship with those who chose to love him back.

In its most basic form, it means that God wants you. Yes, you! We are living in a broken world; I know you feel it. You are living in hurt, pain, suffering, and brokenness. The bad news is that you have messed up and play a role in the brokenness, but the good news is that God wants you in spite of your mistakes. He does *not* attach your value to your flaws. You can always tell the value of something to someone by what someone is willing to pay for it. You were worth enough to God for him to die. You see, God is not just an angry old man in the clouds. Nor is he a God who does not serve justice and wrath. God has wrath for evil and he will deal with it. But scripture is clear that he does not enjoy dolling out wrath and he has offered you a way out. A way to access his kingdom. He does not desire only the smartest, or the most religious, or the most perfect ones. No, God simply wants you just the way you are. He will change you, as he changes all of us, but who you are now is valuable, known, meaningful, and has a purpose to God. He wants you.

I have only scratched the surface of everything I could talk about. I have merely laid out the foundation on which each issue can begin to be addressed. Without a proper foundation to start from, I could never dream of solving any issue at all. I will leave you with a quote that I partially quoted earlier in the book that I will fully quote now. I think it is a good one to sum up not only the gospel, but what the point of the Bible, and subsequently our existence, is truly about:

> If you are a follower of Jesus you should be willing to do what Jesus did. Well what did Jesus do? He was willing to die for his enemies. The greatest being willing to die the worst death ever devised by humankind. That's what He was willing to do. Do you follow Him? Do you love your enemies enough to do that for them because that's what it means to follow Christ. If that's how you see the world and that's how you understand people then you have understood the Gospel. Then you have understood your purpose here. Then you have understood the Christian message. Your life is not your own.
>
> Your life is to be lived for others. You don't have to worry about where your food or clothes will come from. Jesus said that quite clearly. You don't have to worry about where your food will come from, or where your clothes will come from. Don't even the lilies of the field have clothes and the birds of the air food? Don't worry about that stuff, your life is not about that. If your enemy is hungry give him something to eat. If your enemy is thirsty, give him something to drink. He didn't just tell us to do that. He showed us that by living the most humble life.[9]

9. Qureshi, "My Journey to Christ."

Where Were You?

Many of us, myself included, can be tempted in the heat of hardship to focus on our current situation, but when we look at the grand scheme of life, we realize that suffering is temporary. Trials are hard, so when I say that life is good I do not say that lightly. In nearly losing everything, I have gained the most important things. I have time to spend with my family, friends, and loved ones. I have time to tell others the good news that despite the trials we endure, it is only for a brief moment in time. Eventually light will overcome the darkness. Now, this sounds all nice and dandy until you are in the midst of hardship. It is hard to convince yourself when you or a loved one has cancer, or when brutal things happen such as murder, rape, cheating, poverty, injustice, or pain, or even when small trials stack up and you are just having a bad day. In the midst of suffering, it is hard to see how in the world it could be justified. That is why I want to take a moment to address suffering as a whole.

The number one question I have been asked since I left the hospital is the question of suffering and its role in our lives. More specifically, I have been asked how it is possible that a God who holds himself out as being all good could allow such evil and suffering in the world. When considering Christianity, I find that this is a real holdup for people. I cannot pretend to have the perfect answer to this situation, but I do have a response that hopefully can provide some clarity to what I think is not only a logical question but a deeply emotional one. You see, this problem of evil is often presented to me first as a logical argument against God, but it is important to always remember that when you answer a question, you are never just answering a question but you are really answering the questioner.

As I dive deeper into the life of the person who asks this question, I always find that there is some suffering that the questioner has experienced. Perhaps their parent passed away from cancer, or their brother experienced some type of injustice, or their sister some form of sexual abuse. The point is that this seemingly logic-based question is packed with raw emotional needs that need to be addressed as well, and I take this question very seriously. One questioner posed these thoughts: "If there is a God and he is all-powerful, why must there be evil?" "Where does God appear during pandemics, social unrest, and injustice?" Now please keep in mind that what I am sharing I am not claiming is the end-all response, but rather my thoughts and suggestions as I think through these questions.

Here was my response to the above questions:

> Your first two questions are very similar but I will address them separately. I believe the response to the first blends into the second. Both deal with the problem of evil, which is a very logical place to go when, as you have said, there is an all-loving God that Christianity holds out to be real and true. You phrased the first question in a very interesting but I think intelligent way—if there is an all-powerful God, why *must* there be evil? The very fact that you recognize that evil exists, or are at least able to conceptualize that things are not right in the world, is a very important insight that many often do not come to realize. For example, with the cancer in my body, a Hindu, who believes that everything that exists quite literally *is* a part of the divine, would see no wrong in my cancer, or in my death, because it is all a part of God. An atheist too might claim that there is great injustice and wrongs in this world but an atheist, who believes that the whole show is by chance, shouldn't be able to say that a thing is wrong or right; it is simply the way it is.
>
> But clearly, Christianity claims to have an all-powerful God while also claiming that there is evil in the world. How can this be? Or, as you put it, why *must* that be the case? To answer this, I will need to quickly make sense of a few things that often in our Bible Belt culture can be forgotten or watered down to the point where they are meaningless. The first is the truth that God is love. This is so often repeated in both right and wrong contexts that it often loses meaning, but it is vital to remember that love is who our God is. You asked why there must be evil and the answer, simply put, is so that love can exist. You see, who loves another—the arranged marriage where the pair are forced together or the one where both make a choice? People joke around with Siri to see if she will claim to love them, but the reality is that even if Siri said the words "I love you," we know it is not true love, or at least not how we define love. It wouldn't be love because, after all, Siri is just computer programming; she has no choice but to love us or not. It is not a perfect example,

but I hope you can see what I mean. You see, love cannot exist without the ability to not love, and that is the crux on which all of this rests. Because God wants to be with his creation and for his creation to love him and be in a relationship with him and to experience all of the benefits love offers, he must offer the alternative option. Rather than forcing us into a relationship with him, he offers the choice, because that is the only way love can exist.

One of the first responses I hear to that argument usually runs along the lines of, "Well, if God allows evil then either he must not be all-powerful, or he must not be all-loving." At face value, this is a fair statement. How can a loving God look at evil and allow it? Or is the evil countering God so powerful that it is an equal response, and therefore God is not truly all-powerful? Let me respond to that statement by offering an illustration. Right now I feel warm, so I have turned on the cold. Now, anyone who deals in air conditioning will tell you that there actually is no such thing as cold. Cold is the result of a lack of heat. To heat a building, one must create heat and funnel it into a room, but one does not create cold; you are simply taking the heat out of a place. Likewise, the same is true for God, good, and evil. Typically, we think of evil as its own entity, usually embodied in the form of Satan. But this is not the case. Rather, evil is the absence of love. Sin is "missing the mark" of God's standard. It is the opposite, the absence of God. Just as the presence of heat brings its opposite—cold—into existence, so does the presence of good things such as love bring the possibility of evil things such as hate into existence. If heat were not present, neither would cold be, but also neither would the joys of knowing what heat is and what it offers. God wants us. He does love us and wants us to experience that love with him, but in allowing that to be possible—for us to be more than mere programmed robots—we have to have the ability to choose to love and not love.

This is where I will dive into your second question, which is one I can tell has a lot more weight than the first. I know that you are a person of justice. Just from following you, I can tell that you can see that there is right and wrong in the world. You know that murder, injustice, pandemics, holocausts, etc. are wrong. But before I offer my response, I want you to think for a moment about why you think those things are wrong. It may seem cruel at first to think about, but without any God, how can one assign any real worth to a person, and at that any real right and wrong? For example, myself. If there were no real meaning to my existence, one must wonder why I would go to such great lengths and much financial burden to keep myself alive, if all I am is a meaningless accidental blob of atoms, here for a time and gone the next. You could say it is to better the world, but that does not satisfy me if I know this world will one day become dust and everything done here will be meaningless. And if everything is so meaningless, then who cares ultimately what I do or say along the way? We believe racism is wrong, and the Christian response to why racism is wrong is that every person has been made in the image of God and every person is loved, wanted, and valued by God. Without God, people have no real lasting meaning. We can invent some meaning, but ultimately it will fade away. The same goes for morality, or right and wrong. If I believe that killing a person because of race is wrong, but you think it is okay, how do we sort that out? We cannot decide amongst ourselves because we conflict, so we would refer to a higher power, maybe the law. But oftentimes the law of a nation can be wrong, and if it has changed so much, then surely there is no true way of knowing if the law at any time is correct now. The only way then to know is to appeal to an unchanging law that is above both of our authorities.

That was a long paragraph that simply stated this: you know there is right and wrong, and that people have meaning, but I think it is worth it to chew on why you think that is the case. Now, from a Christian perspective, where does God appear in times of suffering? If he hates evil so much, why doesn't he end it all? I think it is both a hard but good question that many have wrestled with over the years. In fact, you'll find that many of the writers of the Bible asked the very same question, thousands of years ago. The reason that God does not simply intervene now is simply stated in two places: the first is in the book of Second Peter, which says,

> The Lord is not slow in keeping his promise, as some understand slowness. Instead he is patient with you, not wanting anyone to perish, but everyone to come to repentance.[10]

The second reason appears in the book of Matthew, chapter 13. We can also observe why God doesn't bring judgment now in a story that Jesus tells, where the owner of a field has his workers plant good seed overnight but an enemy mixes up the good seed with the bad. In the morning, the servants ask if they should tear all the seed up, but the owner replies to wait, because in ripping

---

10. 2 Peter 3:9, NIV.

out everything they might tear up some of what would have been good. So he said to wait until all the plants have grown up to the right time and the sorting will be done then. Now some interpret this passage to be specifically talking about the church, but the premise remains the same. Good and evil are coexisting for a time as God draws more into his kingdom, but it will all be set right in the end at the proper time.

I think these are very powerful statements that give us some insight into what is going on beyond us. The first is that we often look at things from a narrow perspective. I have seen this much more now going through cancer than ever before. Oftentimes we ask God why he doesn't end our suffering now and make it all go away, and it isn't until later that we realize how much he has moved people to come to him through bad situations. I think of the story of Joseph. He was betrayed by his own family for doing no wrong, sold into slavery for no reason, put in prison on a false charge, and spent seven years there with no promise of ever leaving. However, God chose to work through Joseph, and eventually he had a position of leadership and saved his own family. When he finally faced his brothers again, the very ones who started his suffering, he told them, "You intended to harm me, but God intended it for good to accomplish what is now being done, the saving of many lives."[11] Often in our short time on Earth, we fail to see the big picture. We often see God as loving and so think he should heal us now, and we forget that while God wants us healed and whole, he is much more concerned with where we will spend our eternity. It is no good for me to be healed of cancer and extend my lifetime by a few more decades if it keeps me or anyone else from knowing God. I will be healed and whole for an eternity, so what is cancer to me in this short amount of time? I know that it is being used for good because I have seen it being done already.

Because we have rebelled against God, I think it is often important to remember that death, sickness, pandemics, and hate should be all we experience because that is what we deserve for choosing not to follow the literal embodiment of goodness and healing and love. But it is equally important to remember that despite what we deserve, God still has every intent on setting things right again. He began doing so on the cross, the way he proved that he was not a Father content to watch the suffering of people on Earth but a Father who quite literally suffered and died with us, and he will set it all right again. He allows evil for

11. Genesis 50:20, NIV.

now, but it is important to remember that the reason why he waits is not because he intends to sit idly by but because his purpose is to have as many as possible come into a relationship with him. But one day justice will be served. The wrongs will be corrected. So even though we may not see it now, we can have full confidence that God is not idly standing by. Unlike any other religion, God did not watch his children while they suffered, but he suffered to allow the option of a life with him.

Please do not think that I am minimizing suffering in my response. Believe me, I know that life is not always rainbows and unicorns and that there are very dark and terrible things that occur. But what I am saying is that there is a purpose to the hardships. When we ask these hard questions, we often want to know specifically why certain things happen. We want to know why our child had to go through cancer, why a friend committed suicide, why there was rape, why there was abuse or neglect or a child born with deformities, or why we had to go through poverty or the host of other trials of this life. I cannot say I have an answer for all of those problems in everybody's situation. What I do know is that for those in Christ the suffering endured is not meaningless, and that while we may not always get to see specifically how God is using it for good, he has proved time and time again that he does use evil for good and so I can trust that my trials are not in vain.

I do not know all the answers, but, as I said above, I would go through the hardships and pains of cancer for the rest of my life if it meant that someone else could get to know God, because I will have an eternity where I will be whole. Temporary hardships mean nothing to me if someone else gets to know their creator because of it. I think this is where perspective plays a large role in how we handle suffering. It is important to remember that God never promises to take away our suffering in this lifetime, but rather he promises to equip us to endure it through the strength and hope he gives us.

You will notice that I have taken very little time to address the opposing viewpoint, that there is no God, and that suffering is meaningless but rather simply just a part of life. I have taken so little time because the implications are quite simple. Outside of a God and any true meaning to life, there is no point to suffering and that is simply that.

What Is Truth?

"What is truth?" Thousands of years ago, Pilate uttered these words, and he has not been alone in asking since then. I wanted to take a brief moment to address the truth because I believe that there is a concerning trend within postmodern Western culture to personalize truth. Truth is something I had to wrestle with and wrestle with quickly after my diagnosis. If the worst-case scenario happened and I did die, I realized that I needed to settle what truth is. Luckily, I had not waited until the last second to sort out what I believe and I merely had to reexamine my foundation, as I do almost daily, to ensure that what I believe is correct. When it comes to the truth, the phrase you will often hear is "It's true for me." Now, this shouldn't be confused with the phrase "Find your truth." The latter has to do with finding your "authentic self," a philosophy that has issues, but I am not going to address them here. Rather, the idea that goes with the phrase "It's true for me" is that there is no real truth and that we must all make up our own. This concept is known as relativism. The idea of relativism is defined as the belief that "Truth is relative either to the individual or to one's culture or society."[12]

The tragedy is that people read that statement, think about it for a second, see it is a good idea, and accept it without really beginning to think about it. Any good Philosophy 101 class can easily disprove relativistic reality and morality: it simply does not work. We do not say that the answer to "What is two plus two?" merely depends on our point of view, but we like to do this with abstract concepts like morality. The issue with the idea of relativistic morality is that even without considering a God, it cannot be true. To kill someone is either right or wrong. Now, you can say that its morality changes according to a context—war, self-defense, etc.—but in each situation it cannot be both correct and incorrect. For example, we can debate whether or not it is okay to kill someone in self-defense, but we cannot say that it is both right and wrong at the same time. That is impossible. To

12. Borrowdale, "Truth, Reality, and Knowledge."

believe that all truths are equally valid is a colossal contradiction. A friend and I were having lunch today and talking about the Holocaust. Now, if all beliefs were valid, then one must claim that both the belief of the Nazis that the lower races should be exterminated and the belief of the Jews and others that their life had value have equal merit. But that is impossible. It is impossible for those two beliefs to coexist. One must be correct. Some would say it is the one with the most power, but that is just the belief system that gets its ideas played out. However, you would be hard-pressed to find someone who believes abusing a slave is right even though the master has power. Or that the rapist is right even though they have the power. So power is not the determining factor of what is right and wrong and true. If it is not based on power, and if all ideas cannot be equally true, then what is truth?

Relativism shows up in religion as well, especially in the concept of universalism. The idea comes from the belief that at its core all religions are slightly different forms of the same thing or the concept that all religions can coexist. This again is foolery. I can respect someone who is an atheist, who believes the complete opposite of me, more than I can the one who says that all religions are true. The person who says this has not truly examined religions at all and they can certainly not coexist. Now, we can live together and treat one another well. I'm not saying that's impossible. But Christian beliefs are not compatible with Muslim beliefs. All religions cannot be true. Some truths may persist from religion to religion, but it would be laughable to look at atheism and Christianity, or Islam and Buddhism, and say that they are both true. There either is a God or there is not. Christ existed and was who he said he was or not. Muhammad was right or not. The Egyptian sun god Ra is either real or not. Some may get it more right than others, but only one teaching can be true. C. S. Lewis uses the example of math.[13] Some people may get closer to the correct answer to an equation than the others, but getting closer doesn't make their answer correct. There is only one correct answer to a math equation, and while it may be easier to throw your hands up and say there is no answer, as I certainly did in Calculus 1, that does not negate that there is a correct answer out there. It just may take some effort to get to that answer.

The reason relativism is so popular is because it is easier, especially when we are in an argument with someone. We commonly hear the phrase, "Well, you have your opinion and I have mine." That statement typically ends an argument and directly appeals to relativism. It is easy. It is much harder to sort out truth. You have to put in more effort, but that work is necessary if knowledge of the truth is ever to be attained. Here I am not laying down what I believe the truth is and making you abide by it. Many

13. Lewis, *Mere Christianity*, 35–36.

people have been hurt when others force their beliefs on one another, but if I am truly following the Bible, it is not my job to twist arms. Rather, I want to dispel the notion that there is no truth. Clearly, there is truth. I am either sitting in this chair right now or I am not. Both cannot be true. You are either reading this right now or you are not. Both cannot be true. Either there is a God and, further, there is Christ, or there is not. Both cannot be true.

Some have agreed that there is truth but that it is impossible to know what is true outside of personal experience. This is my response:

> If truth were such that it did not exist for certain outside of one's own existence, it would render a person unable to operate in the world. Say, for instance, as the person I was conversing with did, that unless it is experienced, it cannot be true for certain. Let me illustrate it using an extreme example: 9/11. I was not born when 9/11 happened, nor was the person I was having this conversation with. The only way I am aware of 9/11 is through the testimony of virtually every American adult I know and through the video footage shown of the event. However, can I be 100 percent certain that 9/11 happened? Well, by the definition of truth we are using, no we cannot. We cannot be certain that the average American adult isn't lying, that the footage hasn't been doctored, and even that the family members who claim to have lost loved ones on that day actually lost them in those towers. However, if you walked down the street today and told someone 9/11 wasn't real, most everyone would pass you off as a lunatic. Sure, it is possible all of it was fake; I never experienced it. But I have faith that 9/11 happened.

That is what faith is. It is not blindly accepting anything that fits my narrative of reality, but rather trust in the unknown based on facts. While a physical representation may not exist, one still believes the truth to be such. That trust leads you to act on what you believe is true. By claiming 9/11 isn't real due to the lack of the known, a person is actually placing greater trust in the unknown. That person is trusting in the very thing they are disqualifying 9/11 for. Historical evidence is enough for us to accept that 9/11 happened, and there is no great debate amongst us. One could lie and claim it never existed, but the historical evidence would prove that man a fool. Now, I am sure that with time many will claim that 9/11 never have happened at all. That is what is happening, although not in mainstream circles yet, with the Holocaust, and it hasn't even been a hundred years. But lack of belief in 9/11 would not take away its existence. Either four planes crashed into the Twin Towers, the Pentagon, and nearly the White House, or they did not. There is no middle ground.

This is what the Christian says about the life of Christ. Could it all be a hoax? I guess. But the evidence against that probability is so overwhelming that it would be a crazier leap of faith to not believe in the events, however improbable they might be. The historical evidence and actions of the eye-witnesses do not make the case for a hoax. Either a person named Jesus existed, died, and rose again, or he did not.

Some might try to retreat to a middle ground and say he was a great teacher or throw their hands up and claim to not know. In the first case, it is nearly impossible to see someone who claims to be God and see them as lying but still a good moral teacher. No, he is either God or a lunatic. A man on the street can tell me to love my neighbor but as soon as he claims to be God I will immediately regard him as foolish, unless, of course, he can back it up.

To the middle ground of throwing your hands up in resignation, I understand why the position is appealing. One could say, "Well, perhaps 9/11 did happen, but perhaps it did not. I will never know 100 percent for sure, so I will operate without planting my flag." This is the position of the skeptical theist towards God. It seems like it is reasonable and a proper way to go about life, respecting both sides and being content with not being right or wrong. And perhaps this would work for a time. Besides, I don't need to know for certain whether 9/11 happened in my daily life. But this is not the case with God. If you do not plant a flag on its truth, or its falsehood, then you cannot make any other claims about life. Not just in regard to religious things, but to everyday life. Your worldview, and especially the Christian one, permeates all aspects of everyday life.

Take morality for example. A Christian might say which things are right and wrong, while an atheist might say there is no right and wrong except what we pretend to call good and bad. An agnostic would have to stay out of the argument altogether. But you cannot. If a person murdered your sibling or parent or child, you would want justice to be done, but we cannot even talk about justice if morality is relative, and morality can only be objective if there is a law above personal opinion. We may debate on what that standard is, but we must agree that the standard exists at all before we begin the debate. This is just an example of how ignoring the question of religion by staying indifferent will not work in the long run. If you do not say yes or no, then you are relying on yourself. And I think it can be well proven that human self-autonomy breeds chaos. If what I think is good or bad clashes with your idea, then what do we do? You might claim there is no such thing as good or bad, but few people truly believe that, and fewer still live that ideal out. It becomes quite dangerous when they do. I encourage you, dear reader, to seek out the truth because it does exist. And either it gives meaning to all and changes everything, or Christians should be pitied above all.

The Author

I now want to take you back into the midst of my cancer diagnosis. Within those first two weeks, when we did not know what my outlook would be, I was facing the reality of having no control over what my future would be. I had a lot of plans for my life. I had planned to go to college and get my degree and meet some good friends along the way. I had planned to marry someone and to raise a family together with her. I had planned to work hard to get a job and to work hard in that job until the time came for me to retire. I had visions of what myself as a father would look like and what raising my children would be like, both the good and the bad. I saw myself growing old and then, once I had lived a good full life, I would pass away. But the reality staring me in the face now was that those might not be a possibility at all.

I spoke earlier about what I went through in facing death. I will go further now. In facing death, I had to surrender all of those plans and visions that I had made to God. I had to swallow the hard pill that ultimately I am not the one who has the plan for how my life should go. It is not like any of those desires I listed above are bad. I think everyone when they are young has some sort of similar outline for their life and we all have that shattered at some point in our lives. I shared earlier in this book an email that I sent to a pastor. I shared one half of it talking about my mentality in facing death, but I want to share the other half as well:

> I have had to learn to give all pieces of my future, my career, my want to get married, to have a family, completely to God because I do not know if those are things I will get to experience.
> There are many who have been in a similar situation, and many who have gone before me who encourage me. I rest in peace because I know that regardless of what happens to me over these next few months that God is using this to impact people for His good. I have been able to see that already.

One area I had to give to God is infertility. Originally, I was going to omit it from this book, but my mother encouraged me to include it. It is not often talked about in cancer battles and is unfortunately a likely side effect of many powerful chemo drugs, like the kind I have had. While we have preserved a way for me to still be able to have children in the future, I still face a battle that many cancer patients and couples face silently. I want children, but I know that my genetic line now has an increased risk of cancer. It was hard for me to decide—in mere hours—whether I wanted to even have the possibility of children, but ultimately I wanted that chance. I do not know what the future holds in regard to having my own children, but the possibility of being a husband and a father is one of the biggest things I've had to surrender. I do not think there are many more beautiful things than to be a parent, but I realize that even that is no longer in my hands and I have had to once again surrender.

It is not easy to surrender. I wanted the certainty of those things I have listed above very badly. I still do. I very badly want to find someone who will love me and whom I can love and serve. I want to have children, to watch them grow up, and to be a father to them. I want to grow old and experience all of the ups and downs that life may bring. But ultimately that is not guaranteed for me. I do not know whether my life has months, a few years, or decades left for me. I am grateful for all the time I have had, especially now when I look back and realize how close I was to not making it out of January 2021. I wake up every morning and thank God for it. I really do, because none of my days are guaranteed. They are a gift. Every interaction I get to have with my family, with my friends, is one that I get to have that I was not entitled to. It is hard to surrender. But it is rewarding to do so. I think I explained it best in the speech I gave before I was baptized. I had to omit much of what I was going to say due to time, but I still have my rough drafts. This is what I said in those omitted notes:

> I have realized now that looking back over my life I have seen how God was showing me how little control I have and how much I need God. You see constantly throughout my life, often without realizing it, I have placed my trust and purpose in things that don't last. Throughout my life I have asked why I had to grow up with little money, why my parents had to be apart, why my plans for my future were drastically changed, and why people in my life left.
>
> I've realized that what was going on was a years-long dialogue between God and me ever since I was seven. Me saying God you're real but my real foundation is in my family. God showed me that it wasn't. God, you're real but I'd be happier with

more money. No, you wouldn't be. God, I think you're real, and also I have these plans for how my life is going to go. I know exactly where I'll go to college and then I know the job I'll get and I'll have a family and I'll live a long lovely life. God had different plans.

What I've realized is that every moment in my life has been me trying to hold onto and control things that were out of my control and things that were temporary. God has been saying, give me your family, give me your finances, your plans. But God can't I still hold onto my life? That future that I wanted? No God's shown me, even those are His to control.

And what I have seen each and every time that I have surrendered those different areas of my life is that they are better off in His hands than in mine. His plan for my life looks a lot different than the one I had, but the end result has been much more beautiful than I could have ever imagined. I would not trade a second of my life. Because every time there has been hardship, there has been something beautiful that has come because of it that would not have existed if that hardship hadn't occurred.

To surrender control is not easy, but I have a Father who cares for me. His ways are higher than my ways. Sometimes it takes a lifetime to see it, and some may never see it in this lifetime. But this is what Jesus meant when he spoke of denying yourself when the Bible speaks of dying to oneself.[14] When you surrender every fiber of your being—all of your plans, all of your views of other people, all of your old ways of thinking; when all of what makes you who you are is surrendered—and you let Christ take away the broken pieces, when you let Christ run the chemo through you, he fills you up with himself and who he is. When you decrease and he increases, it changes everything. I do not have to convince you that life will bring hardships and suffering. God has this peculiar way of bringing each of us to the breaking point where we realize that who we are is broken and not enough. Some try to hold on to who they are. I chose to surrender myself. To let go of Matthew. It was only when I surrendered fully that I was able to experience true peace in the midst of the storm. There are few who sum up this concept of surrender better than C. S. Lewis in his closing pages of *Mere Christianity*:

> When you have completely given yourself up to His (Christ's) personality, you will then, for the first time in your life, be developing into a real person. He made the whole world. He invented, as an author invents characters in a book, all different men that

14. See Matthew 16:24–26.

you and I were intended to be. Our real selves, are so to speak, waiting for themselves in Him.

What I call myself now is hardly a person at all. It's mainly a meeting place between various natural forces, desires, fears, etc, some of which come from my ancestors, some from my education. Some perhaps from devils. The self you were really intended to be, is something that lives not from nature, but from God.

At the beginning of these talks, I said there were personalities in God. Well, I will go further now. There are no real personalities anywhere else. I mean no full complete personalities. It's only when you allow yourself to be drawn into His light that you turn into a true person.

But on the other hand, it's just no good at all going to Christ for the sake of developing a fuller personality. As long as that's what you're bothered about, you haven't begun because the very first step to finding yourself is forgetting yourself.

It will only come if you are looking for something else. Even in literature or art, no man who cares about originality will ever be original. It's the man who is only thinking about doing a good job or of telling the truth that does something original. Even in social life, you will never make a good impression as long as you are thinking about making a good impression.

That principle runs through all of life from top to bottom. Give up yourself and you will find your real self. Lose your life and you will save it. Submit to death, submit with every fiber of your being, and you will find eternal life.

Look for Christ and you will get Him and with Him, everything else thrown in. Look for yourself and you will only get hatred, loneliness, despair, ruin.[15]

---

15. Lewis, *Mere Christianity*, 225–27.

The Eternal Perspective

I talked earlier about my new perspective after being diagnosed with cancer. When I was first diagnosed, I was secretly a little determined to not change because of cancer, but the reality is that it is too life-changing to not be changed by it at least in some way. I wanted to take a moment in this chapter to tie everything that I have been talking about previously together. I spoke separately about suffering and perspective, but the reality is that they go hand in hand when Christ comes into the picture.

You see, I truly believe that the reason we struggle so violently with our suffering is because it is not what we were intended to experience. Our rebellion has brought it on, but there is an idea, as Paul writes in Romans, that all of nature groans for its creator.[16] He uses the language of a woman in labor pains to describe the state of the world in separation from its creator. We need our creator. The opposition we feel against the death, decay, pain, depression, and suffering that we experience should at least clue us in that something with this whole operation is not right.

My parents have had to walk through pain that is unimaginable shy of losing me. I hope that they never have to experience that. Still, the pain of having to watch their child suffer—and being helpless to do anything about it—is more difficult than I can put into words. When you or your loved one has a chronic illness, it never goes away. You have good days. You have bad days. You have days in denial. You have doctor's checkups, but even if they go extremely well, it is only a reminder that that illness is still there. Your life is consumed by it. When you do lose someone, or when trauma strikes, your life is consumed by the pain and by their absence. You just want a few moments back with them.

Now, I cannot pretend that I know any answers to pain and suffering, but I do believe as a Christian that the enemy wants us to be consumed by our suffering. Instead of viewing it as our temporary cross to bear, the

16. Romans 8:18–23.

enemy wants us consumed by the drowning feeling we often get, to be all-consumed by our situations. As a follower of Christ, I remember that in reality all suffering is temporary. Even an atheist thinks that. But I realize as a Christian something that the atheist does not: through my pain, God can take what is evil and turn it for good. The suffering I endure is only momentary when compared to what eternity will be like.

We hate suffering. My parents, I am sure, would give up all their possessions, sacrifice their own bodies, even their own lives, if it meant that I didn't have to experience this. I think we forget sometimes that God feels that way too. Even more. We hear so often about how God sent his Son that it loses its meaning. But what does that really mean? It means that feeling of pain you experience when you suffer, that willingness to give everything to protect your children, God feels that more. He feels it so much that he came down in the person of Christ to die. And not just to die but to suffer, and suffer far worse than I have. I refer again to the note I wrote before my baptism. On that note I wrapped up by saying:

> And even though right now it is hard to even walk, even though some days I cannot even stand up without tremendous effort, and even though my body is sick, there will be a day, really not that long in the future, when I am whole, healed, when I can run freely, and when I am home with my Father. And even though I have suffered I know that I serve a God that was not content to sit on his throne and watch his children suffer but came here, suffered far worse than I have, in order to be with His children.

We often look at our suffering through the lens of the present. And it is hard not to. Anyone who has experienced physical pain will tell you that it is hard to not concentrate on anything else in the moment. However, when we step back and look in hindsight or when we look at things from the grand perspective of God, when we look at the big picture, we can begin to see that though the pain hurts now, there is an eternal goal that far outweighs my temporary suffering. Yes, I may want to be healed now, to be financially wealthy now, to have all the pleasures of life now, but what good is my being healed now just to prolong my life if I or someone else misses out on what really matters? If it takes my temporary suffering to bring someone who would otherwise not have known Christ to him, then bring it on. I will have an eternity to be in my healed and whole body. Yes, God wants us healed and whole, but as Christ says, "What does it benefit a person to gain the whole world but forfeit his soul?"[17] Christ never once

17. Mark 8:36, NASB.

promised that by following him life would have less pain and fewer hardships. Rather, quite the opposite. What he did promise is that behind the pain and suffering there is him. I want to look at things from that eternal perspective.

It Is Well

At the beginning of this book, I set out to share my story in the hope that it might help others, and that you, dear reader, might find some inspiration and strength through my experiences. This book has only encompassed the lessons I have learned in one year. There are eighteen more years filled with triumphs and trials, which I have hardly mentioned here. Now at this conclusion, I want to take one final moment to say that while I certainly do not have all of the answers, I do know one thing. I know that despite all the isolation from COVID, despite the long nights and early mornings, despite the painful biopsies and the weakness cancer has caused me, despite the needle sticks and nausea, despite the chemotherapy and the loss, despite the divorces I endured as a child and the pain of losing people in my life that I have loved, despite the long nights of loneliness and the days of depression, and despite all of the other pains and suffering I have endured, I would go through it all again in a heartbeat if it meant that you knew our Father. I do not say this lightly. It has not been easy to go on this journey, but it would be worth it.

I also recognize that there are people out there who have suffered far worse than I have. I hear the stories of other people who have gone through cancer and those who have endured far worse than I have. This is not a book where I say, "Woe is me." Rather, I truly believe that I have nothing to complain about. I don't. I have been blessed with healing, and with a lot of side effects on the table that I could have had to go through. I have seen the beauty that has been there amid hardships. I count myself as very fortunate.

I don't know what kind of brokenness you have experienced in your life. I don't know if you are going through COVID or its effects, through cancer, through a broken body, through loss of limb, through anger or a head injury, through embarrassment or humiliation, through feelings that you are meaningless or worthless, through loneliness or depression, through rape or abuse, through infertility or miscarraige, through addiction or poor parenting, through trauma or soul-crushing stress, through loss of house or car or life, or if you are just having a bad day. I may not be able to answer why you are going through those things, but there are truths I do know.

I know that there was a person called Yeshua (Jesus), who loved you so much that he was not content to leave you broken but has invited you into his kingdom and paid your debt. Because of that, I know that you have meaning and worth and purpose. Because of him, I know that your suffering can have meaning and will not be wasted. Because of him, I can look at my journey through this past year as I have endured the impact of COVID and cancer through Christ, and I can smile and know that whatever life situation comes my way, I am safe in my Father's arms.

What I have experienced has been hard and I am sure that I will experience further if not deeper hardships in the future, but because of him I can do as I did the first week when I was diagnosed. I stood there in the shower at one of my lowest points and I sang "How Great Thou Art." I know that he is greater than Matthew, and because of that I can look at any life situation and not just tolerate it but have joy through it. I can experience his peace, and I can say that it is well.

> Therefore we do not lose heart, but though our outer person is decaying, yet our inner person is being renewed day by day. For our *momentary*, light affliction is producing for us an *eternal* weight of glory far beyond all comparison, while we look not at the things which are seen, but at the things which are not seen; for the things which are seen are temporal, but the things which are not seen are eternal.[18]

---

18. 2 Corinthians 4:16–18, NASB.

Bibliography

Borrowdale, Jeffrey. "Truth, Reality, and Knowledge: The Correspondence Theory of Truth." January 21, 2019. https://media.lanecc.edu/users/borrowdalej/phl203_w19/phl203_w19_handout_0107_truth_reality_knowledge_1.html.

Chan, Francis, with Danae Yankoski. *Crazy Love*. 3rd ed. Colorado Springs, CO: David C. Cook, 2015.

Lewis, C. S. *Mere Christianity*. New York: HarperCollins, 2017.

Qureshi, Nabeel. "My Journey to Christ." Lecture delivered July 20, 2014. Video recording available at https://www.youtube.com/watch?v=2bjv2t7PC7E.

www.ingramcontent.com/pod-product-compliance
Lightning Source LLC
Chambersburg PA
CBHW071050090426
42737CB00013B/2312